DREAMS

Unleashed

DREAMS

Unleashed

You Hold The Key

CLAUDETTE SNOW

BRIGHTFLAME
Books By Experts

Published in Canada by BrightFlame Books, Burlington, ON.

First Edition © 2017.

ISBN (eBook): 978-1-988179-31-5
ISBN (Paperback): 978-1-988179-32-2
ISBN (Hardback): 978-1-988179-33-9

DEDICATION

Tom and Sue Reed—If not for you I would never have witnessed the true art of living life, as it is meant to be.

*You have inspired me to chase my dreams,
open my heart and face my fears.*

I am eternally grateful for the day you came into my life. You have filled my heart with love and set my soul on fire. You have made me want to discover the best version of myself.

You clearly caused something that had been sleeping in me for years to reawaken. I am nervous, anxious and afraid but guess what? I'm going for it anyway. What's the worst that could happen?

I'm going to find out who I am and why I'm here. I am on a journey to find my purpose. We all have one, and this book is proof that I am making tremendous progress.

No two paths in life cross without reason. I believe you were brought into mine so I could change it.

TABLE OF CONTENTS AND AUTHORS

INTRODUCTION

The first purpose of this book is to fulfill my own dream of producing a valuable piece of literature. The second, is to share it with millions around the globe, to prove what can be accomplished in their own lives. I want to help people grow, see their full potential and reach it. I would like to make a positive impact on those who want or need to change their circumstances.

I would like others to be aware that there is a process available to help anybody become the person they wish to be. I know because I did it and I believe in it. I am not alone in my quest to find purpose. My co-authors have graciously agreed to share their own experiences of transformation.

This book is the first volume of a long running success series. A compilation of true life stories by those unafraid to release the past and create their own destiny. People with the courage to overcome life's obstacles and create the future of their choosing. They offer hope, strength and inspiration to others allowing them to realize, having in one's possession a burning desire, faith, persistence and determination, every dream imagined can be obtained.

1

FINDING MYSELF

By Claudette Snow

You must be willing to let go

"Letting go is part of moving on to something better. You will not get what you truly deserve if you're too attached to the things you're supposed to let go of. Sometimes you love and you struggle and you learn and you move on. And that's okay. You must be willing to let go of the life you planned for, so you can enjoy the life that is waiting for you."

UNKNOWN

How did this happen? How did I get so lost? How did I lose myself? Where did my dreams and aspirations go? These are just a few of the many questions I'd asked after waking from a nap, that had lasted almost ten years.

I remember feeling terribly afraid and very confused. I looked around my beautiful home ever so slowly, as if in a fog. I loved everything I saw and yet I knew that something inside had snapped. The realization had hit me hard with a furious blow and I had no choice but to confront it. The truth was, I simply was not happy.

I felt like a fool, like a failure, like a person coming out of a coma. I suddenly became conscious of the fact that I had no clue how I had gotten here. I walked around and looked at family pictures. My heart filled with love and pride as I studied the faces of the people who share my daily life. They are kind, smart, funny, and very attractive.

I felt such a sense of guilt for not feeling ecstatic. I felt gratitude but I didn't feel joy or fulfillment. I tried to push the feelings aside, though I knew I couldn't hold them at bay forever. I was in such denial of my situation, my circumstances and my entire life. I wondered how I had ever made it this far fooling myself, not to mention everyone else around me. As I continued to roam my surroundings, I caught sight of myself in the mirror and at that moment I knew, there was a total stranger looking back at me.

That day was the beginning of search… to find out who I was… who I am… who I want to be and why I'm here. Feeling very alone and dissatisfied, I sat in a chair and began talking out loud to myself. I asked, "What do I want and how do I get it?" I knew I had to make changes but I didn't know where to start. I didn't feel I had anyone in my life who could help me understand what I was going through.

However, I was a huge believer in prayer and every night I would lay in bed and ask for answers and guidance. After being continuously met with silence, my frustration only mounted and out of desperation I screamed in anguish begging for direction. Strange how things happen. For it was only a short time after my meltdown when help arrived in the form of a long lost friend.

He had contacted me on social media and suggested we meet in person. I was quite nervous and apprehensive about going as we hadn't seen each other in thirty-five years. I figured I had nothing to lose and I was right. That meeting had forever changed my world. We reminisced about our pasts and discussed our futures. It was a very uncomfortable conversation for me because I had no clear vision or direction of where I was going. My friend had dreams, goals and a very clear plan set out for himself.

I was very impressed that he had been able to overcome so many challenges and turn his life into a tremendous success. My intuition was telling me that this meeting was no accident. I just knew that my old friend showed up right at a time that I desperately needed help.

No longer feeling alone, I swallowed my pride and shared my hopes, dreams and fears. His response was, "I can help you fix everything." I thought this was a rather strong, not to mention arrogant statement for anybody to make. I also knew I had to take a chance because clearly, I wasn't doing a very good job of making the life I wanted.

I met with this gentleman a few more times and listened to what he had to share with me. I realized he knew things about me that I didn't know about myself. He knew lots of things.

Every time we got together, my belief in him grew and I just knew that he could and would do everything that he said. I knew it was time for me to accept the help being offered. I needed to find out why things were happening in my life. I needed to know that I had control of my decisions and that my future depended on me and nobody else. I was so ready to find myself, to really start living and not just exist.

I am so happy and grateful for the day an old friend came calling. Pay attention, it wasn't an accident. I was pleading for help, I asked for it out loud. You know the old saying, "Be careful what you wish for, you might just get it?" My wish was granted in the form of a friend. One who is highly trained and experienced in life. One who has overcome tremendous challenges and defeated adversity. A person who continued to search for the answers to a better life, until he found them.

The fact that he was willing to share his knowledge and training with me were a blessing. I would have paid anything to find the happiness I truly longed for. What my friend taught me was, how to think, and how to think into the results I wanted. I have never looked back. The education and information that I have received is serving me far beyond anything I ever learned in the traditional school system. I was fascinated to realize that everything I ever wanted was already here. I now know that I have the ability to control all things in my life by using my own faculties.

I have learned about a process that has changed my world and I continue to put it to use every day. Since learning how to think in a manner that benefits me, I have become much stronger, confident and daring. In truth, I have found myself. I am a happier person having understood the laws that govern our being.

Now that I have discovered the best version of the person I always hoped to be, my journey carries me further into deeper meaning. The meaning of my purpose and who I'm meant to serve. Deep in my heart I know what my purpose is. It has been screaming at me since childhood but I chose to ignore it, because I never had enough faith or belief in myself to accept I could actually achieve it.

That's all changed now and I am going to live my dreams, my life and my purpose on my terms. So just remember when you send a plea, a prayer or request into the universe, the answer may often be delivered in the form of an old friend who comes calling.

> "A master in the art of living draws no sharp distinction between work and his play; his labour and his leisure; his mind and his body; his education and his recreation. He hardly knows which is which. He simply pursues his vision of excellence through whatever he is doing, and leaves others to determine whether he is working or playing. To himself, he always appears to be doing both."
>
> LAWRENCE PEARSALL JACKS

2

MY JOURNEY TO PURPOSE

By Claudette Snow

"Until we learn to love ourselves and recognize our worth, we can never truly add value to the lives of others."

CLAUDETTE SNOW

Morning comes early when you have something to look forward to. You know that excitement when you're going on vacation or you have a special occasion? Most people don't fly out of bed energetically looking forward to greeting the day and all the experiences that come with it. In fact, most people I know absolutely dread waking up and starting their usual routine. Doesn't seem to matter if it's a well paying, high ranking career or a day spent nurturing children. Nobody seems completely happy with the choices they've made for their lives.

Fortunately, I am no longer one of those people but I used to be. It took many years before I realized that I wasn't actually living my life. I was simply going through the motions of daily responsibility. To the outside world, it appeared my life was perfect. I seemed to have it all. Everything anyone could ever want and more, except what mattered most to me....happiness. It took tremendous amounts of soul-searching and self-evaluation to come to terms with the truth.

It's quite a testament to how my life had spiralled out of control when I wasn't looking. As bad as it may appear, this list—which you can see on the page opposite—was the best thing I had ever done. I highly recommend everyone take the time to write their own.

After reading my findings for what seemed like the hundredth time, it was as if I'd been clobbered over the head and could finally see light again. The most valuable lesson I learned was the very last thing I had written, FEAR. There staring back at me was the answer to every problem I'd ever had.

The next revelation was accepting the fact that I had nobody but myself to blame. Being afraid to rock the boat was not a quality I was proud of. Realizing the toll it had taken on my life, it was certainly something I needed to rid myself of.

I always thought that going along with the crowd and conforming to what others expected of me would lead me to a full and peaceful life.

I couldn't have been more wrong.

MY FINDINGS

- I only seem to surround myself with negative or toxic people.

- I never knew how to say, "NO" to anybody.

- I never did anything nurturing for myself.

- I always put the wants and needs of others before my own.

- I never felt accepted or good enough.

- I believed every bad or terrible thing that was said about me.

- I no longer had self-confidence.

- I was ashamed to share my feelings for fear of being judged.

- I woke up every day feeling tired and depressed.

- I no longer thought about the dreams I'd once had.

- I felt unappreciated and unworthy.

- I felt hopeless and stuck.

- I had lost belief in myself.

- Fear that things could actually get worse kept me trapped exactly where I didn't want to be.

I was filled with anger and rage that the world had moved on without me, and the worst part was I had allowed it to happen. I knew the only way to alter my path was to change my way of thinking. I had to be consciously aware of my thoughts and also the choices I made.

I was at a point where I no longer cared about fitting in, or what anyone else thought about me. I decided to cleanse my life of all negativity. I took back the power that never should have been relinquished in the first place. I can't tell you how liberating it felt.

I needed to take a good look at the company I was keeping. None were bad or terrible people but LORD, most were quite miserable. I made a choice to distance myself from the doom and gloom.

Not surprisingly, I didn't miss anyone too much and I found myself attracting much more positive influences into my life. When asked to do things for others they could clearly do for themselves, I made a conscious choice to say, "NO." The other person wasn't always happy with my response but that was their problem, not mine.

I really started to pay attention to my feelings, thoughts and actions. I was finally participating in my own life and it felt empowering. The sky didn't come crashing down if I said something that didn't make everyone happy. I started doing things on my own for myself and every day seemed to be such a gift. I came to realize that bad things happen to good people over the course of a lifetime. My advice would be, "Deal with it and let it go." We cannot change the past, it's happened. All we can do is focus on the things we have control over and that's ourselves. Whether we respond or react to something is our choice.

Deciding to stay in a situation or walk away is something only you can decide for yourself.

People often forget it's their life they're living. They become so obligated feeling it's their job to make sure everyone else is happy and taken care of. They find themselves left behind while building the dreams of others. The more time I spent alone thinking about the person I used to be, the more my confidence grew. I knew I had to give myself a second chance to be the real me, to live my life for me and nobody else!

I forgave myself and everyone else that I held responsible for my stagnate years. Once I had done that, it seemed the weight of the world had been dropped from my soul. I suddenly felt so light, happy and energetic. I was motivated and inspired to start my new life. I knew that I would never allow the darkness of negativity, self-doubt or especially fear, to enter my thoughts again.

The dream I had carried in my heart since childhood was to be a writer. I wanted to give hope, strength, and inspiration so others would realize all they are capable of, as long as they keep believing and never give up. Every experience is meant to teach us something about ourselves. Perhaps I was meant to lose myself for a time in order to rediscover my happiness, passion and true purpose. I was not living the life I was suppose to be because I was living for everyone else but myself.

Life is meant to be lived in a certain way, from the inside out... not the other way around. Once I stopped allowing people and outside circumstances to affect me, my entire world changed. I took my life back.

I learned that only I could control my thoughts, feelings, and actions. So, what was I going to do with this new found knowledge? I was going to put it to the test. I was going to see if my desire mixed with faith could actually turn my dream into reality. And now... you are holding proof of my belief in your hands.

> *"What lies behind us and what lies before us are tiny matters compared to what lies within us."*
>
> RALPH WALDO EMERSON

3

MANIFESTING MOTHERHOOD

By Deborah DeJong

"Whatever the mind can conceive and believe, it can achieve".

NAPOLEON HILL

Am I crying? Why in the world am I crying? Where are these tears coming from? How could this be possible? I was sitting on a beautiful Caribbean beach feeling the warm sand between my toes, while a cool, salty, breeze gently tossed my hair in the wind. Some people would have said I had it all...a great job, solid friendships, a loving family, my ideal weight and a healthy abundant lifestyle including a fun convertible! On the outside, everything appeared wonderful, but on the inside, something felt "off." Something was missing, but I couldn't articulate this missing link.

On the beach that day, the beautiful, billowing, clouds gently floated by in the sky, but they seemed to be carrying something off with them. It was a message. Was it for me? What did they want me to know? "Wait," I called. "I am listening! I am open to receive whatever it is I need to know to live a more fulfilling life and my best life! What am I missing?" I waited and listened and the answer was revealed.

The universe did have a message for me that day, and the clouds were indeed carrying something away with them. It was my number one dream and deep felt desire. In that moment, I realized what was going on. I realized that it was one thing to lose the dream of a fairytale white wedding with prince charming, but it was completely different to lose the dream of being a mom. The pain was so deep that it cut to the sacred core of my being. The tears weren't just flowing out of nowhere, they were completely related to the realization that at 35 it wasn't just the clouds rolling away that day, it was my long held desire and purpose in life. And in that blurry moment where I could barely see the clouds anymore, my vision became crystal clear.

I made a decision that would forever change the trajectory of my life. I made a decision to do absolutely whatever it would take to become a mom. I knew I would confidently look at myself in the mirror one day with no regrets, knowing I had done everything I could possibly think of to manifest my dream. I had no idea how I was going to do it. I just knew I was going to do it! I was going to be a mom. It's funny how blurry eyes can actually lead to clear and flawless vision when you are open to receive.

Wayne Dyer, the famous author of *10 Secrets for Success and Inner Peace*, encourages us not to die with our music still in us. He states, "the music that you hear inside of you urging you to take risks and follow your dreams is your intuitive connection to the purpose in your heart since birth"(p.32). I experienced the music that day and decided to listen and act. I started to dance my own dance.

As I sat there letting the reality of this decision sink into my entire body, I quickly realized a decision of this magnitude needed a strong support system. But who would be part of my 'tribe'? As I thought about which family and friends to share and explore my dream with, I felt terror. I felt anxious and fearful of their potential reactions and how their feelings and thoughts might impact my decision and our relationship. I recognized that my fears could get the best of me and derail my dream completely, so I chose to focus solely on my decision. My decision was made! My decision was clear in every aspect of my being; mentally, emotionally, physically and spiritually. I utilized the power of my will to avoid any distractions, noise or negative people. I was going to be a mom or at least die trying.

My decision has reminded me of a story by Napoleon Hill, in *Think and Grow Rich*. He wrote about an army commander who was leading his men into battle against a powerful enemy. When their boats landed on shore before the battle, he instructed his men to burn the boats. Can you imagine? He told his men they either win or die, but they would not be leaving or retreating. His troops burnt the boats... and then they won. People who are forced to win or die usually win. That is exactly what I did! I burnt the boats. I wasn't turning back. I truly had decided that it did not matter if friends or family disowned me or chose to end the relationship.

If I wanted to be free and at peace, I had to be 'me.' Not the me that others thought I should be, but the "me" that I knew in my soul I already was... a mother. I called my family doctor and as the saying goes, "the rest was history."

As I write this now, the tears flow again. Partly, in remembrance of that deeply sad "knowing," (when I was sitting on the beach watching the clouds dance by in a perfect blue sky that I was about to miss out on my deepest desire), but also with a deeply appreciative heart (listening to the giggles of two gentle souls engaged in a playful tickle-fest in the next room). I'm so lucky that they are mine (and I tell them every day). I don't know where I got the strength everyday to proceed and keep moving forward. But, it was always there.

Remember—when the pain in your soul cuts so deep (and you might even feel the tears streaming down your face), yet you cannot articulate where they are coming from or why they are here, then be still (take a deep breath). Listen, (for the answer is already here). Ask, (the universe is always listening to your every desire). Reach for the clouds, (have faith that it is never too late). Believe, (that you are worthy of all your desires). Allow, (the universe to deliver your desires in the perfect time and space). Receive, (be open to receive with a grateful heart).

It never ceases to amaze me that the Eskimos apparently have over 80 words for snow, but in our English language we only have two words to express our deepest felt gratitude, and those two words are "thank you." Thank you for being you and sharing your best self with the world.

In the end, having followed this strategy and emotionally attaching to my goal of manifesting motherhood, I have learned a very valuable lesson. A lesson that is not just about life, but about love. It is a lesson I now share with my children. I have learned that the greatest gift we can give or receive in this lifetime truly is LOVE. Love is "my" best life. Love is "your" best life. Love is "the" best life...and we know this for sure. When fear and love arrive at your door, choose love. It may be a person, an experience, a calling or a way of life. How are you giving love today? How are you receiving love today? We only have today so I encourage you to love more, live more, dream more and always dance.

When we ask the universe to manifest a dream, and we believe with the power of deep and compelling faith, and then proceed to be completely open to receive the gift and allow the universe to deliver, the gift will arrive. Maybe not at the exact time or date or the exact way or shape we had imagined. But the dream will arrive. The moment I clearly asked, with loving conviction, my little ones were already on their way. And they aren't so little anymore!

Together we end our day in pure love and deep gratitude with our family prayer ritual saying "God Bless Mommy... (and we continue listing all our family members) and for all the special people in the world, who make our dreams come true." Because they do!

"When you get the chance to sit it out or dance...I hope you DANCE".

LEE ANN WOMACK

Deborah DeJong is a proud single mother by choice with two beautiful and creative children.The universe blessed her with both a boy and a girl. She is a loving mother, inspirational life coach, motivational author, compelling speaker and successful entrepreneur. She is the author of *DANCE: Five Steps to Living your Best Life*, which was a book written that led to her decision to pursue her dream of motherhood.

She is the strategic CEO of Deborah D Coaching offering online courses and coaching for individuals and groups around the globe who wish to live their best life through using her DANCE model! Her core program, Pursuing Parenthood serves professional women and couples who are eager to start a family.

Visit **www.deborahdejong.com** for more information regarding this inspirational woman and the divine services she offers to the world!

4

THE IMAGE WE PROJECT
By Don Weimer

"When the image that we present to the world doesn't reflect how we truly feel inside, we need to take action to eliminate that conflict."

DON WEIMER

There are a lot of us who have been living lives as two different people, the one we present to the world and the one we present to ourselves. I have spoken to many people about this and we have agreed that this is quite normal. This is how I have felt inside, for as long as I can remember.

I was raised to believe that working hard and being successful was very important. That is where your energy was supposed to be directed. Part of a successful persona is a happy home life and that is what you try to project.

I have lived this "two-life" facade for the past 30 years. I have attained success in my professional life and I have a beautiful wife and daughter. A storybook life, right? Maybe to the outside observer, but not to those closest to me, or myself.

I was unhappy for the majority of the last 30 years, and I was making those around me unhappy as well. I could not tell you why my life was like this, at least not until now.

We have all heard stories about individuals who seemed to have it all, success, a beautiful family, wealth and admiration. This is what they projected to the world, and for some reason, they would still go off the rails. There are numerous examples of successful people struggling with addictions, destructive behaviour or their light is extinguished in desperation, through suicide.

I remember hearing a quote from Elvis Presley, many years ago, that for some reason resonated with me. Elvis said, "the image is one thing and the human being is another... it's very hard to live up to an image." This quote made sense to me, because this is exactly how I was living and I truly struggled with finding happiness.

In the Fall of 2015, I made a decision to find happiness. Little did I know the magnitude of the emotional journey I was going to experience. I learned that if I wanted to be happy I had better learn who I really was and why I thought the way I did. I needed to learn why my inner voice was constantly talking to me about things that had nothing to do with my idea of what "success" was supposed to look like. Why was there such an internal conflict in what I was thinking, versus what I was doing? You see,

I had convinced myself I was not worthy of all I had achieved, or all the wonderful things in my life.

When your inner voice tells you that you are not worthy of the love or acceptance you have in your life, your behaviour will make sure personal happiness will never be attained. This concept caused me to dig deep, into my paradigms. *Paradigms are a collection of habits, you were programmed with at a very early age.* It is not as important to understand how you developed your particular paradigms, but it is critical to recognize they are present and they are in conflict with personal happiness.

My paradigms had me believing that I was not a good person, I did not deserve Love and I was constantly seeking the sympathy of others. Having limiting beliefs like this automatically caused me to do things that proved my beliefs to be true. I did not recognize my paradigms and therefore I didn't know why I was behaving in such a destructive manner. *I was doing things that I didn't want to do and they were giving me results that I did not want to get...* and I didn't know why, but I kept doing them.

There are two ways to replace old, negative paradigms with new empowering ones. The first is called an *"emotional shock."* An emotional shock is a significant event that has a profound impact on you, right to your very core. Emotional shocks are almost always negative in nature. The second way to replace limiting beliefs is through *"constant spaced repetition."* Read the same thing, write the same thing, over and over and over, until it becomes fixed in your mind. The new paradigms will eventually overtake the old, negative paradigms causing your behaviour and your results to automatically change.

It was very hard to look in the mirror and see my reflection looking back, knowing that behind those eyes was a person who was sad and hurting. Hurting inside and hurting those around him. It was harder still to take action to change my paradigms. Taking action meant that I would have to change. I would have to give up all the things I was doing, that kept me tethered to my limiting beliefs. I would have to learn to love myself, rather than loath myself.

The route I took to seek happiness included both, an emotional impact and spaced repetition. The emotional impact was the potential of losing everything good, in my personal life. The old me would have let it all slip away because that would just be fulfilling my old paradigm… I'm not worthy of receiving it, so it makes sense that I would lose it. I had to clearly identify my limiting beliefs and I would have to replace them with the polar opposite, through repetitive affirmations… spaced repetition.

When I embarked on the journey to replace my limiting beliefs it was one of the hardest things I have ever done. I studied myself, identified my beliefs and developed a number of affirmations designed to help me finally love myself.

As I began my affirmations, I knew I was on the right path, based on the emotions, or the internal conflict that presented itself. *"I am a good person and I am Loved, I am accepted and I forgive myself."* Simple words that had a massive emotional impact on me. I took this affirmation and repeated it out loud, over and over. I sat down and wrote it out 20 times per day, for 30 days in a row. The strangest things started to happen. At first, every time I did my affirmations, I was reduced to tears. This idea that

I was a "good person," who is "worthy of love and happiness" was in complete conflict with my deeply rooted belief.

As I pushed on with my affirmations, I started to behave differently. The things I used to do to justify my old beliefs, were no longer being done. I became more patient. I started to learn how to talk about my emotions and was able to have meaningful discussions, with those closest to me. I began to Love myself, for the very first time in my Life!

"I am a good person! I am Loved! I am Accepted! I forgive myself!"

As I write this, the image that I hold in my mind regarding my future, is one filled with happiness and I am surrounded by the Love of my family. For the first time in my life, I can hold a picture in my mind of a happy, love-filled future.

There is a very simple formula, that can lead you to everything you desire. First, identify what is holding you back, then make the **decision** that you are committed to changing your **limiting beliefs**, the last step...**take action!** We all have the ability to create our own environment. Imagine your life filled with an abundance of love, joy and happiness! My journey is proof that anyone can achieve happiness in their lives...Including **YOU!**

"The "self-image" is the key to human personality and human behaviour. Change the self-image and you change the personality and the behaviour."

MAXWELL MALTZ

Don Weimer lives in a small town, in Southern Ontario, with his beautiful wife and talented daughter. He has worked in the Food Industry for close to 30 years. His passion lays in the creation of high-performance teams through professional development and coaching of team members. Each team that Don's had the privilege to work with has delivered record-setting results. Don has received "Expert" training in the Theory of Constraint and has attained his Level 3 certification in Green Belt Six-Sigma, Continuous Improvement. As well, Don has been committed to ongoing cultural changes, in the area of Food Safety, and has been recognized as a leader in this field.

5

PASSING ON THE BLESSINGS

By Cheron Kovacs

Dedicated to Caylee, Kendra & Kera.
Don't be afraid to unleash the greatness within you!

11 *"For I know the plans I have for you," declares the LORD, "plans to prosper you and not to harm you, plans to give you hope and a future."*

JEREMIAH 29:11 (NIV)

Why today matters

"Today is not just an ordinary day. Today is a day that matters. Today you will have the choice to make a difference in your life and those around you. Today you will have the chance to smile rather than frown, be grateful, rather than selfish, lift up rather than tear down, accept rather than reject and love, rather than hate. Today you will have the choice of seeking hope for the future or remain in the hopelessness of the past. Today you have the choice to laugh or cry. Both will make you feel better. Today you will have the undivided attention of the King of the Universe. At that time you can ask Him anything you want. You can ask for help, plead for a friend or just enjoy His presence. It all depends on you whichever you choose, today matters. Make the choice to make it a day worth living. And don't forget, tomorrow is another day." - Tom Krause

I was born & raised in Zimbabwe, Africa. I am the oldest of seven siblings. Growing up, I never had much confidence in myself. I was independent in the fact that I worked and lived on my own, but I still relied heavily on my family. When I was 23, I had my eldest daughter out of wedlock. The relationship with her father did not survive. I was absolutely devastated by the break up. Our daughter was only one-year-old.

I was fortunate to have the love & support of my family, and one of the most amazing bosses. I remember crying in his office on countless occasions. At one point, I even contemplated killing myself, but couldn't do it. I felt I couldn't leave my daughter without a mother, giving that responsibility to someone else. I am so grateful that I chose life for both my daughter and myself. I soon realized that her father was not the man for me. We were not meant to embark on life's journey together.

A few years later, I met another man, with whom we came to Canada. After being together for one year, the relationship dissolved. Prior to moving out of our family home, I had a vision of myself standing on a stage giving a speech to a large audience. At this particular time, I did not have the faith I have today. I certainly didn't believe in my abilities to achieve such a goal, so I ignored it.

I wasn't working, so my daughter and I went to live in a shelter. After arriving I called a very good friend, (who I refer to as my sister). I told her where we were and she immediately sent her husband to retrieve us. They told us that as long as they had a home, we would always have a place to live. It was through the generosity of these amazing people that I gave my life to the Lord. Through them, I learned the beauty of sacrificing for others, pure heartfelt love and kindness.

It is here in Canada that I began to realize how truly dependent I was on my family. This is where I believe my transformation began. I started growing in small ways that I wasn't initially aware of. I also had a, "box mentality" which I held onto for so long! When I look at the person I am now, I wonder why I did that to myself, but all is not lost. If I hadn't been that way, I wouldn't be here today, writing my story to encourage others. Canada is where I began my journey to true independence, finding my faith, becoming self confident, as well as believing in my abilities to achieve the goals I have set.

For many years, I lived my life as a single parent. I faced a number of trials, some easier than others. I never allowed those trials to keep me down. I had to keep striving for my daughter. I made the sacrifice to stay in Canada for her future. Although my heart sometimes wished to return home, I was changing and was afraid that if I went back, I would once again become reliant on others. I certainly didn't want to be that person again. I am eternally grateful that I made the decision to remain in Canada, because today I'm growing into an individual that I truly love!

At some point, I started to wonder what my life's purpose was and how I would achieve it. I knew so many people who'd realized their calling and were striving to attain it. I desperately longed to find mine. Not long after, a friend recommended I read a motivational book. I truly loved it. From here, I started to believe in myself in very small doses. I would do well for a little while, but my old way of negative thinking would always creep back. However, I didn't give up and continued to study as many motivational books as possible.

After six years on my own, I finally met my soul mate. We married, started our family and were very happy together. Suddenly, I was faced with my greatest challenge, a horrific family crises. Initially, I was angry with the Lord and the universe for the injustice.

I spent two years filled with pain and grief before I decided to look for the positive in this situation. I chose to count the many blessings I had. As soon as I did, things started to change. I realized that all the trials I had faced were moulding me for the person I need to be. My confidence slowly increased and once again I started changing my way of thinking. I began to see that every situation has a positive or negative outcome and we have the choice of deciding which one it will be. I chose to be thankful for the thorns in my side.

Immediately after attaining an attitude of gratitude, amazing things started to transpire. My heart longed to find an opportunity which would allow me to work from home and care for my children. I desired a career that would positively impact the lives of others. My intention was to pursue this goal in the distant future. Unbeknown to me, my positive attitude was attracting phenomenal opportunities for me.

I was presented with a business offer and because of it, I was connected with a Motivational Speaker. Immediately I had the same vision from years prior. It was me standing on a stage addressing a large audience. I then realized that my purpose is to be a Motivational Speaker who inspires others to reach their highest potential in life.

My greatest change came when I was introduced to an amazing gentleman, who told me he could help me continue on this journey of growth, as well as connect me with many like-minded individuals. I knew I was ready for this new adventure, so I took him up on his offer. I am well on my way to a very bright future.

I am learning how to remain positive in a negative world and I am truly happy. I am being connected with so many phenomenal people who have attained great success and continue to do so. I am fulfilling my purpose of helping others. I know that I have much to learn, as well as much to give.

The positive changes I have made in my life are having a ripple effect on my family and others around me. My oldest daughter keeps telling me how proud she is of me. Our relationship is improving vastly, another great desire of my heart. My younger daughters are responding to me better (I am still a work in progress in this department, I have to admit, but I am getting there). Two of my sisters are encouraged by the events of my life and are taking steps to improve their own situations. It is liberating to be able to pass on my blessings.

> *"He who refreshes others will himself be re-freshed."*
>
> PROVERB

Now that I have found my purpose, and gotten rid of my "box mentality" I am pursuing my goals with a vengeance! I feel alive and have discovered I have many talents I wasn't aware of. It is awe-inspiring to experience the unfolding of oneself. It is encouraging to know that there are people out there who are making a difference and I am now one of them.

Know that whatever difficult situation you face, is preparing you to be the great person you are destined to be. Be thankful for that thorn in your side. By changing your way of thinking, you will attract all that you desire.

Start today by looking in the mirror, tell yourself how beautiful you are. Do this as often as you can. Initially, you might feel silly doing it (I did), but now I love going to the mirror and telling myself I am beautiful! Start believing in yourself, see your potential and start taking those steps to living your life of purpose.

If I had only changed myself first

When I was young and free and my imagination had no limits I dreamed of changing the world. As I grew older and wiser and realized the world would not change I shortened my sights somewhat and decided to change only my country: but it too seemed immovable. As I grew into my twilight years I settled on changing only my family and those closest to me, but alas they would have none of it. Now as I lay on my deathbed and I suddenly realize that if I had only changed myself first, then by example I could perhaps have changed my family, and from their inspiration and encouragement to me I would have been better able to help my country and from there I may even have been able to change the world.

(TAKEN FROM THE TOMB OF A BISHOP IN
WESTMINSTER ABBEY 1100 A.D).

Cheron Kovacs is from Zimbabwe, Africa. She currently resides in Canada with her husband and children.

Cheron is a student immersed in the study of Personal Development and is aspiring to be a Motivational Speaker. Should you wish to connect with her, please email cheronev@yahoo.ca.

6

THE LIGHT OF POSSIBILITY

By Frank Richards and Trisha Leconte

"A great attitude does much more than turn on the lights in our worlds; it seems to magically connect us to all sorts of serendipitous opportunities that were somehow absent before the change."

EARL NIGHTINGALE

Wake. Work. Exercise. TV. Sleep. Repeat. That was literally our life. Frank and I reflect back on these days when it was normal to do this, in fact, it is normal for most people. Now that we look back, it's amazing to see how far we have come. What allowed us to break away from this pattern and start living the life we dreamed of? It was **attitude** – the magic word.

After my dad was diagnosed with cancer for the second time, I was devastated. To see someone you love in so much pain is heart-wrenching. I remember deciding to be strong for my family. I had to remain positive, so I developed a positive attitude. It comforted me, my family, and others around me.

Even after my dad's passing, I was still determined to keep this positive attitude because I saw how much it was changing my life. Why was everyone around me expecting me to feel down and depressed? I love my dad and miss him dearly, but I chose to focus on the good. I chose to believe that he is in a better place. I chose to remember that his last year of suffering gave me the opportunity to love him and make him smile each and every day. It was my attitude which kept me strong, afloat and focused on all the good around me.

I started to understand that I was in control of my own feelings, and that's when I started to break away from the crowd. I remember Wayne Dyer asking how can anyone hurt your feelings? They come from your thoughts. Then I remembered Viktor E. Frankl in the concentration camp, where despite all the bad happening around him, he survived because he was able to give himself strength and purpose by controlling his thoughts.

Then it dawned on me. I have the freedom to choose any thought I want and therefore be, do, and have anything I want. My attitude towards life started shifting more and more. My typical response to "How are you?" was "Eh, pretty good." Well, I outgrew that. Now every day is "wonderful." People challenge me, "Is it really wonderful?" I say, "Yes! It really is."

Funny things happen when you spend a lot of time around people. Your goodness starts to rub off on them. My fiancé Frank at the time noticed my wonderful attitude and started adopting it. It was amazing seeing him grow alongside me. Something as simple as attitude can really change your life. It did for us. We went from being left-brained, logical software engineers to right-brained, creative entrepreneurs. And it started with our shift in attitude.

People started noticing us. They started asking what we were doing. They were interested to know how to improve their own lives because they saw a dramatic change in ours.

While most people wait for something wonderful to happen, we create it! Why? It's just our attitude towards life and life gives you back what you put out.

We can only describe a positive attitude as a light that allows you to see life differently. We stopped being lazy couch-potatoes. We started waking up at 4:30 am. Why? So we can read, workout, write our goals, and plan out the day. Most people have a negative attitude toward waking up early, and thus it never happens for them, and they continue to complain they don't have time for this and that.

Our slight shift in attitude started out as a little light and eventually grew. It lit the path of opportunities that we can now see and take advantage of. We attracted so many people, resources, and opportunities that were in line with our goal.

Having the right attitude is the starting point toward making a big change in your life. If you have a great attitude toward something, you're more likely to try it, otherwise, you won't and could miss out on some amazing opportunities. A great attitude puts you in charge because it starts with your thoughts. If you think about it, our thoughts are really the only thing we have complete control over. No one can make you think something you do not want. So as long as you have the right mental attitude and expect to get what you want, you'll get it.

Frank and I need a telescope to see how far we have come. Two introverts who used to hide behind keyboards and monitors are now getting on stages and speaking to the world. Instead of looking at YouTube videos, we're on YouTube. Instead of reading blog posts, we're publishing blog posts. Instead of going to events, we're hosting events. We've been able to create the freedom we've always wanted. Now, we teach people how to do the same.

Our mission is to wake people up. To snap them out of autopilot. To teach them how to understand themselves and make that mental shift to understand that they can create the life they want – that they can be, do, and have anything they desire.

If you want to change your life and start living the life of your dreams, you need to start with your attitude. That will start to shine the light on what's possible for you – but it does start with you, my friend.

Trisha Leconte is the co-founder of Frank & Trisha Coaching Inc. in San Jose, California. She helps people discover their true potential and turn their dreams into reality, their goals into achievements.

She is a certified PGI Consultant and works with Bob Proctor and Sandy Gallagher from Proctor Gallagher Institute.

Before coaching full-time, Trisha was a Software Engineer and graduated with a Master's degree from Santa Clara University. She worked in the corporate field for about 10 years. After getting into personal development, she says making the jump to becoming an entrepreneur was a quick decision.

She uses her coding skills, love for graphic design, and passion for Toastmasters in her business. Trisha transformed from being a very shy, and quiet person, to speaking on stages. Her passion is greater than her fears and that is what keeps her moving forward into growth. Her motto is KEY – Keep Evolving Yourself and that is what she teaches her clients to do.

As a young child, Frank Richards learned the importance of helping others through his family's volunteer efforts for the U.S. military and local families in Germany. His volunteering continued and grew into tutoring and mentoring throughout both grade school and college in Louisiana, where he pursued a degree in technology.

Before graduating *summa cum laude* with a bachelor in Computer Science, he had already secured an IT job in Silicon Valley because of his four internships.

Frank has over 15 years experience as a Software Engineer with several years of management and leading worldwide teams in both development and support. He got into management because he wanted to help people grow their careers and found great interest in their personal achievements.

After witnessing the trends in the industry and how it affects the lives of many, he decided to take a leap of faith to help empower others to take back control of their lives and develop their own economies.

Frank became co-founder of Frank & Trisha Coaching Inc. and is a certified PGI Consultant working with Bob Proctor and Sandy Gallagher from Proctor Gallagher Institute. He wakes up every morning wondering whose life he's going to impact.

Frank & Trisha Coaching Inc.

- www.frankandtrisha.com
- hi@frankandtrisha.com

7

GROW WHERE YOU'RE PLANTED
By Sandy Clipsham

"When the student is ready, the teacher will appear."

- ZEN PROVERB

The shortest email I ever wrote was also the most important. It was just two words: "I'm ready." It took me six months to be ready to decide to make my life better. I knew a specific coach and mentor, a teacher who I could work with. One who had gotten incredible results working with friends I trust. Yet I, the student, sat on my hands for six whole months from the time I first met with him before sending that email.

If that sounds strange, it is strange.

Yet can't we all point to situations where the right decision is there in our hearts and we just keep on coming up with reasons not to go for it? So there I was, finally ready to make a new beginning. From the moment I sent that two-word email, my life has grown immeasurably.

That was January 4th, 2016. And since that day, I have found a lot of answers, because I have been willing to go looking for them. That has been uncomfortable at times, because it has exposed some of the holes in the way I'd been thinking, and nobody really enjoys holding that up to the light. Even those six months of agonizing over the decision to reach out to a mentor are short in comparison to the 20 years it took me to line up my beliefs with my actions.

While in university, around 1996, I was active in a student entrepreneurship organization called ACE. The ACE conference in Toronto that year featured a keynote by Verne Harnish, one of the organization's founders. Harnish is a master storyteller, and gave one of the best presentations I'd ever attended.

In his address to students, Harnish told the story of one of the founders of the tea-making company Celestial Seasonings, who started his company by experimenting with different flavour combinations and selling the blends to local health food stores. This man, Mo Siegel, built it into a multimillion dollar company and then sold his interest. Following the buyout, Siegel was travelling the world, in some effort to rediscover himself and what he would do next, given that he had no obligations or financial constraints.

In India, he had the opportunity to meet Mother Teresa. He told her he was trying to figure out what to do next with his life, whereupon she jabbed her finger into his chest emphatically while stating simply, "grow where you're planted." What that meant for Siegel was a return to the tea business, expanding Celestial Seasonings in his second stint as CEO, a period perhaps even more successful than the first.

In telling the story, Harnish drove home the point to budding student entrepreneurs that it's important to stay true to your deepest interests, to keep you going through the tough times of starting and running a business. The message resonated with me because at the time I was in an academic program. I didn't care much for, "science" and was trying to sort out my next move.

When I got home after the conference, I was unable to sleep because I was mulling over that speech. I got up, went to the kitchen cupboard, thinking that I could have a cup of… what else but, Celestial Seasonings tea. As I opened the box, there was a quote on the tab of the packaging that caught my eye. It was from poet Muriel Rukeyser: "The world is made of **stories**, not *atoms*." Remember, I was a science major at the time and it was the closest thing to an epiphany I have ever experienced.

"I knew in that moment that I needed to somehow be working in the "story business."

That dawning led me to enter the career counselling profession, where I worked for many years. If you think about what a good career counsellor does, it is to assist others in shaping their stories to reach their career goals. It's fair to say that I spent much of the time working on the goals of others, though not much time on my own.

In fact, up until recently, the last time that I did a significant amount of work on myself and my true goals was during that period twenty years ago, following the entrepreneurship conference. After that, I just put my nose down, finished my degree, got married to my true love, and took advantage of some opportunities that came my way. But if you'd asked me at any time, "Are you growing where you're planted?" I doubt I would have said yes. I reached a low point after a conflict at work meant having to leave a good job behind.

Then, in 2008, I had another awakening at night, only this time it wasn't from dwelling on a speech about entrepreneurship. It was crying in the next room. I had become a father. Corrina is a joy. She is thoughtful and smart and creative like her mother. She once said, "you know what? All the hugs and kisses we have fill my tummy right to the top with love – so full it erupts with lava like a volcano." I found that by observing her learn and grow and share love, I wanted to make myself better too. It's clear to me now that to find my true calling, I needed to first become a father.

Prior to that, I don't think I understood just how deeply we want our lives to matter. Let me explain with another bedtime anecdote, this one from my three year old son Wesley. My wife was singing a lullaby that both my son and my daughter have heard many times: "You are my sunshine, my only sunshine." He interrupted, "mommy, am I your sunshine?" Yes sweetie. A pause, then "is Corrina too?" Here he was, wanting to know that he mattered and trying to square the line, "my *only* sunshine" with the fact that his sister gets the same lullaby.

It is part of the human condition that **we want our lives to matter**. I had to understand that before I got into my life's work, saving family stories through personal history documentaries. I didn't know it at the time, but the story Verne Harnish had shared all those years ago about Mo Siegel's encounter with Mother Teresa is a great example of Siegel's own "personal history."

Through the company I founded in 2013, **Forever Tree Films**, I capture many truly inspiring stories from people who have lived very full lives. I have been hired by families to sit down with their elders, some of whom went to school in a one-room schoolhouse or came to Canada on a ship with a single suitcase housing all their worldly possessions.

I get to ask really interesting questions like: "how have you changed the most since you were 21? What advice would you give to your younger self? How do you want to be remembered?" So, I've listened to these beautiful stories of pain, love, struggle, overcoming, failing and succeeding. It's a great challenge to distill all that into a documentary film that honours each one's unique legacy. That challenge keeps me grounded.

"When the student is ready, the teacher will appear"

Those words echoed in my head when I sent that two word email, "I'm ready" to my mentor back in January, 2016. My results ever since have skyrocketed, thanks to him and my Mastermind partners who have helped me grow beyond the beliefs that were holding me back. I've made some great friends, I'm growing my business, and

I'm shattering the paradigms that say, "you can't do that!" – the ones that have a way of keeping us from living the life of our dreams.

In short, I'm experiencing all the magic that happens when you grow where you're planted.

Sandy Clipsham uses video to share personal and corporate histories. He has always been drawn to the art of the interview, first as a career counsellor, now as a personal historian who created Forever Tree Films www.forevertreefilms.com.

He has an insatiable curiosity for uncovering the "thumbprint stories" that best express an individual's story and honour their legacy.

Once while watching his kids on the playground, he met a man with a 100-year-old mother, who attributes her longevity to sardines. He has been eating them straight from the can ever since.

8

MEANINGFUL MOMENTS

By Karen Gordon

"Today I will let my light shine in hopes of lighting the way for others."

KAREN GORDON

Shortly before my 50th birthday I realized I had been living a lie. I had been a conscientious student, found a job and had been working very hard. I had been playing by the rules or at least what I perceived the rules to be. The problem was, after all of my dedication, I was nowhere near my financial goals. I also wasn't living with passion, knowing I had yet to find my true life path. I had come to the conclusion that I needed to start working smarter not harder.

The initial turning point happened one day when I was extremely frustrated. I blurted out loud, "Enough is enough! I am almost 50 years old. It is time for me to discover my calling and do what I was meant to do!" I said and felt this with strong, **heartfelt emotion**. Although tying an emotion to a request is one of the key steps of manifesting, at the time I did not know that so I did it due to sheer exasperation. Shortly after that, events started clicking into place like pieces of a puzzle. I had asked for what I wanted and now it was time to receive.

I was offered and accepted a job in the personal development field. This was an incredible opportunity because I am passionate about self improvement. Along with my new career, a new way of thinking was also introduced. I began to re-evaluate my views. What if the **beliefs** in my mind were not necessarily true? Just because I had believed something for a long time doesn't make it true. For example, my belief that the only way for me to make money was, find a job and then work hard. I realized that my daily thoughts and habits needed to be re-evaluated. My thoughts, feelings and habits are closely related, and together create my results!

For example, I used to worry constantly. I remember when Bobby McFerrin's song, "Don't Worry, Be Happy" was on the radio. When I would hear the song I very much wanted to stop worrying and just BE happy but I couldn't. Thankfully now I can.

I know now that excessive worrying was such a waste of my precious time and energy. Now I use my mind and time for productive thoughts toward my desires. I practice the following:

1. Visualizing my goal with clarity, detail, and emotion.
2. I then pull the vision into the "NOW," and see it unfolding in the present.

This process has done wonders for me. This new way of thinking has helped me alter personality traits that were holding me back. I am now taking the time and using my mind to create meaningful moments that matter. Time is always in motion, therefore, I am always in motion. Time is moving me forward, whether I want it to or not. However, I can choose my future with focused thoughts. So, I made a conscious decision to grow. These days, I am able to connect to the now and create meaningful, magical moments. I enjoy life's precious moments, because all I really have is this moment right now.

I have been trying to manifest financial abundance for years. Through self study, I was able to recognize that I wasn't feeling worthy of financial prosperity. This is a great discovery because it taught me that I was repelling the financial wealth I was trying so hard to manifest.

I have learned that by continuously writing out positive affirmations, I could overcome my false negative belief about money. I started writing, "I am worthy of great financial abundance." The first time I wrote this, it actually took my breath away! I knew that if my old way of thinking was that deeply engrained, I had to keep writing it over and over again in order to get past it.

I used to think only other people were worthy of financial abundance. I now realize that I am the other people! I am worthy - we are all worthy! We were all born with gifts and talents. We all have a reason for being here. This discovery helped me to stop living small and start living large! The opportunity to become an author and write a chapter for this book, soon followed. I accepted the challenge immediately because my confidence had increased.

Writing is what my soul had been seeking. Writing is my true creative outlet. It is an outlet for my voice and I have finally found it! I found my passion and in turn found my purpose in life! I see infinite opportunities now. I am grateful that I am now on a path of clarity. I give gratitude daily as I know it will bring me more of the same.

Thank you for co-creating this experience with me.

Lasting impressions

"As the fog clears, focus is claimed."

KAREN GORDON

"Into the tide may your worries ride."

KAREN GORDON

"Love and laughter is what I am after. May they find their way to you."

KAREN GORDON

Karen Gordon is a mother and has a wonderfully supportive husband. Her interest in personal development began as she neared her fiftieth birthday. Now that she was a half century old, Karen felt it was time to re-evaluate her life since she was not living up to her true potential. Through personal development she learned to change her mindset, and then in turn, her results changed for the better.

Karen is a now a bestselling author. Karen and her husband Evan have written their story in a book titled, "How My Husband Keeps Me Happy" which is available for purchase at:

www.howmyhusbandkeepsmehappy.com.

9

PEACE

By Sara Jamil

"Change the way you look at things, and the things you look at change."

DR. WAYNE W. DYER

This is the unfolding of my burning desire for peace and the lessons I have learned along the way. It all started in my mother's womb. The sweet nectar of her soul nourished and laid the foundation for my quest for peace.

My childhood and adolescence were nothing out of the ordinary; curiosity, wonder, experimenting, trying to fit in, and figuring out where I really belonged. High school graduation followed with marriage, relocating to a new country, two children and divorce. This series of events meant moving back to my childhood home as a single parent. I worked and studied for a teaching degree, re-married, moved yet again to a new country and had my third child. These experiences challenged me to make difficult decisions along the way, but they were all part of my **self-discovery**.

The pivotal moment came around my 40th birthday, (not a coincidence, if you refer to the "experts"). I often read about people turning 40 having mid life crisis etc. I however, actually started to blossom and live my life. Looking from the outside though, the circumstances at the time in my personal life looked quite the opposite. Those "lessons" became very sacred, as they opened me up to embracing **vulnerability**, (as if my life before forty hadn't taught me enough!). The sudden passing of one of my close friends that year truly **awakened** me. I made a **commitment** to myself to be unstoppable in taking any and every *action* to improve my inner as well as outer world, by not wasting a single breath I was blessed with.

Enrolling in an amazing personal development course that same year, empowered me to create the possibility of "living a life I love and to live it powerfully." First and foremost I learned what it means to live **authentically**. The following quote best describes what I hold dear:

> "**Authenticity** is a daily practice. Living authen-
> tically means cultivating the **courage** to be
> emotionally honest, to set boundaries, and to al-
> low ourselves to be vulnerable; exercising the
> **compassion** that comes from knowing that we
> are all made of light and darkness, strength and
> struggle; and nurturing the **connection** and
> sense of belonging that can only happen, when we
> let go of who we are supposed to be and embrace
> who we are. Authenticity demands **wholeheart-
> ed** living and loving — even when it's hard, even
> when it hurts, and especially when we are wres-

tling with the shame and fear of "not being enough". Mindfully practicing authenticity during our most soul-searching struggles is how we invite grace, joy, and gratitude into our lives."

BRENÉ BROWN.

Turning inwards and checking up on my thought patterns opened up for immense growth in my spirituality and my calling. The thirst to learn more led me to another **personal growth** program, which really amplified the understanding on the power of my mind. I have learned that how and what I choose to think is crucial to how I feel and what I do in life, that it has an impact on those around me. I have learned that I am a thought evolved being, just as everyone else on this planet. I start with a thought, and thoughts are things that I have control over. That's where my power lies. I decide what kind of person I want to be. It's all about **perception**. I am aware that there is a divine, spiritual power that constantly flows to and through me, (through all of us). It resides deep within me and is seeking to express itself, but *my limiting beliefs about others and myself are the roadblocks to my transformation.* The only way for me to remove those blocks is to focus within and tune in to my thoughts, feelings and actions; noticing my self-talk, shifting the negative, judgmental voice to one that is compassionate and loving.

My perception is the source of all my reactions. For example, if someone says or does something, I have a thought, and I react to my thought about what that person said or did. The comment or behavior of that person didn't cause my reaction. My thought did!

I am responsible for my thoughts and feelings. My reaction serves as a red flag to what specific thoughts and beliefs are causing me pain or suffering. Changing my reaction is not just a matter of self-control. That can only help me manage an emotional reaction and a physical one. Understanding and seeing the other person, or even myself through **loving, compassionate** eyes is the *best* way to change my reaction permanently.

We react to what we perceive, so when we change our perception our **reaction** changes automatically into a **response**. This realization has had a profound impact on me. I now have the **knowledge** and **tools** to transform how I see myself, others, and challenging moments. This brings the possibility of huge, instant, and permanent **results**.

If a thought or belief doesn't create joy or peace, it's not the Truth! I have to ask *empowering* questions like, "What would peace do now?" or "What do I *really* want?" It is my responsibility to learn how to develop and *master my mind*, to *take inventory of myself,* and then do some serious inner work over a long period of time with enthusiasm and persistence, so that I am able to respond rather than react to circumstances in life.

All my "suffering" has been a *blessing in disguise*. I see it now as a *lesson in peace*. Although I love to gain knowledge from studying books, I have come to realize that my children are the biggest source of education on compassion and peace. They are my beautiful jewels, each shining their unique light to teach me more about myself.

My ability to respond versus react, has been put to the ultimate test in my capacity of being a mother. I have failed miserably many times; yet have found the **courage** to keep on growing and improving myself, as my children are getting older. The most painful, heartbreaking experiences have been with my eldest, my son. For the past five, long, soul-crushing years, I have experienced the consequences of reacting, of judging, of frustration, of disappointment, of darkness. My son had entered his own unfolding of life and it resulted in our home being out of harmony and peace.

It is only through knowledge and understanding of the principles that I have mentioned here, that I have been able to begin **transforming** my relationship with my son. By **changing my perception, focusing on what I really want, and asking empowering questions**; do I want heartache or do I want peace with my son? By **making a decision** to want harmony back in my family, and then work at it with patience and persistence, I have learned that to be able to lead my children, I have to first be able to *lead myself.*

We all have one life and it really is up to us *how we choose to live it.* I strongly believe that **no soul is burdened beyond what it has strength to endure**. I went from living with a victim mindset to learning to live with a **growth mindset**. Instead of isolating myself from the world in a state of self-pity, while I was going through challenges, I was always pulled towards service to my fellow beings spreading love and joy. That gave me *strength* and *courage* to *persevere,* and it increased my well-being!

The pivotal moment when I made a decision to shift my mindset to the possibility of **being** compassion, love and peace in everything I do, *all day and every day,* I started to attract new opportunities to further develop this potential.

My quest for peace and journey of self-discovery isn't over yet, but this I have learned: Life is a lesson in responsibility, i.e. being able to respond to life; watch it evolve and **unfold**, embrace all experiences, develop **patience** and **calmness of mind**. Learn to **trust** that all is well, no matter what it looks like from the outside. I have learned that peace is what I really want and I am prepared to give my life to attain it. To have it, I must do things in a certain way!

> *"Calmness of mind is one of the beautiful jewels of wisdom. It is the result of long and patient effort in self-control"*
>
> JAMES ALLEN.

Sara Jamil was born in Denmark to Pakistani Muslim immigrants and is the eldest of three siblings. She currently lives in Toronto, Canada, with her loving, supportive husband and three children; Shuaib, Maha, and Aleena.

Sara holds a Bachelor of Education, and is closely connected to her local community by being involved in several initiatives; such as volunteering with the Yellow Brick House (a local Charity working on rebuilding the lives of abused women and children), organizing food drives, hosting Mats of Kindness events (where sleeping mats are weaved out of milk bags for the needy, locally and worldwide).

She mentors young girls in her faith community and serves as School Council Chair at her youngest child's school. Sara is constantly on the lookout to support grassroots initiatives that promote peace and compassionate living.

Last but not least, Sara is the Founder of CompassionFirst, a social enterprise empowering women of all ages to actively engage in personal growth through compassion.

To learn more please visit www.compassionfirst.ca or e-mail Sara@compassionfirst.ca

10

YOUR GREATNESS WITHIN

By Mahmood Sheikh

"In Reality, you are so much more than you think you are…In your Reality, you are no more than you think you are."

MAHMOOD SHEIKH

The fact that you are reading this book tells me something about you. You are an inquisitive seeker. Have you ever noticed that everyone of us, deep down inside, is on a journey to explore? As a newborn child, we begin to explore our new world with an insatiable curiosity and amazement. Taking in all of the wonderful things that we experience, in a state of complete awe and living in the moment. If only we would remain in that state of awe and amazement!

Hello, my name is Mahmood Sheikh and I would like to take you on a journey with me for the brief time we spend here together. A thought-provoking journey of self-discovery. So sit back, relax and make yourself a nice cup of tea. I'll wait for you!

Let me start by telling you a little bit about myself. I was born in Kenya, Nairobi. My father, who worked in the British Railway in Africa had seen pictures of Canada and thought, what a beautiful country so he applied to come here. He also applied for Hong Kong, just in case. Then he prayed and said, "Dear God, take me where it is best for me and my family." So in December of 1965 we landed in this beautiful country, that I now call home. I grew up in Brantford, Ontario which is a small city about an hour west of Toronto. I am one of 5 siblings. I now live in Barrie, Ontario with my loving wife of 27 years and two beautiful twin daughters.

Now, if I were to ask you to describe yourself, you would probably tell me something similar to what I just described. Maybe you would tell me what you do as a career, what is your ethnic background, where you live, etcetera. What happens over time, is that we tend to believe that is who we are. You see everything that I just told you about me, is not who I am. What I described, is merely my story up until now. We play many different roles throughout our lives believing that is who we are. I am not even my name. 'Mahmood Sheikh' is nothing more than my label, so that when my body shows up, you know what to call it! As a matter of fact, before we named our two daughters Shumyla and Zahnab, they had another name. There they were in the hospital lying in their little cradles with a label on each, one with 'Twin A' and the other with 'Twin B.' Can you imagine if we kept that as their names! They would be like celebrities. Like Kanye West's daughter whose name is North!

So the question arises, if that is not who I am, then who am I? I asked a friend of mine to tell me "who are you?" without telling me your name, what you do or what roles you play in life? She pondered this for quite some time and then she said what seems to be very logical, "I am a human being." When you are born, you arrive in a body, when you look in the mirror you see yourself in your body and wherever you go, you go in your body. Let's take a closer look at that. The human body is truly an amazing thing. I'd like you to think about your baby pictures for a moment. When you look at your pictures, do you not look and sometimes wonder who is that? Where is that child? Did you know that almost every single cell that was in your 'baby body' has died off, or been replaced many times over with new cells? Here are some fascinating facts about your body. There are between 50-75 trillion cells in the body. The human brain is the most complex, powerful machine in the Universe that we know. The brain contains a network of about 100,000 miles of blood vessels and 100 billion neurons, with a capacity to perform some 10 quadrillion operations per second. Imagine the scope and complexity of every phone system throughout the entire planet. Your brain embodies that same scale of complexity and capacity in each individual brain cell! Your body is constantly replacing old cells with new ones at a rate of millions per second. By the time you finish reading this sentence, 50 million cells would have died and been replaced by new ones! So if you believe you are your body, then my question to you is, which body are you talking about?

In all of your versions of your body from birth until now, the 'I' is constant. Who is this 'I' that we talk about when we say 'I Am? Take a moment to think about that. Science and technology are so advanced, that when you move your finger, they can track what muscles you use, what nerves are being fired with the electronic impulses, all the way to the part of your brain where the command is triggered. However, they cannot find the commander. You see, who you truly are is beyond your physicalness. Who you truly are transcends your body. You are form-less. You are nothing (no-thing). Wait a minute, are you telling me that I am not my name or my body and that I am nothing?! That's probably what you are thinking right about now. (I told you this journey would be thought-provoking!)

So the question arises again, **who am I?** Have you ever caught yourself saying, "I was saying to myself?" Think about that for a moment. 'I,' was saying to 'myself.' So is that two of you having a conversation? Who is 'I' and who is 'self?' Now that's really getting trippy! Stay with me now, because it's going to get even more wild. Just wrap your head around the first part. So, when I am talking to myself, am I the talker or the listener, or both? Now, this is where is gets wilder. There is that part of you that is talk-ing and there is that part of you that is listening, and behind all of that, there is that part of you that is witness-ing all of that! Read that sentence over again because it is critical.

Who you Truly are, is the witnessing presence behind your thoughts. You are the Observer.

You are not a human being, you just happen to be ob-serving one. Let that sink in for a while. (Your tea is probably cold by now, sorry!)

You may not have heard it put this way before, or maybe you had some idea that there is something more to this experience of life than just our physical existence. In the statement above, it is mentioned that you are the witnessing presence behind your thoughts.

Let's talk a little bit now about your thoughts. Where do they come from? What are your prominent thoughts? What role do your thoughts play? I'd like you to do something right now. Ok, close your eyes (wait, close your eyes AFTER I tell you what I want you to do!) When you close your eyes, I want you to pay attention to your thoughts. Just be aware of your thoughts, do not judge them, just observe them. Do this for about a minute. You will quickly realize that your thoughts are streaming in non-stop! You have anywhere from 60,000 to 80,000 thoughts a day.

Now understand this, your thoughts are invisible, or in the realm of the non-physical. If we were to open up your brain, we would not find a thought. Every single thing that you see in the physical world which we have manifested, first started as a thought in the non-physical. Take a look around you, this book that you are reading, the furniture in your home, the painting on the wall, the shoes you wear, all of these first started with a thought! So, your thoughts come from the infinite field of the non-physical realm. That's where everything comes from. Out of the 60,000 to 80,000 thoughts that you have a day, up to 90% are the same thoughts that you had yesterday, and the day before that and the day before that and so on. If you are having the same thoughts over and over again, can you see how this would start to become a **habit**? Whatever your prominent thoughts are that you repeat over and over again, manifests in the physical world as your life experience!

We are *programmed* to think a certain way at a very early stage in our life. These are the habits that you grew up with. It goes something like this; you are born in a particular family where you begin to identify yourself with your name, you learn about your ethnic background, your traditions, your religious beliefs, social acceptances, and away you go. This programming is passed on from generation to generation. Think about this, if you were born in a family on the other side of the world, you would have a totally different life experience. You would have a different set of habits and beliefs, and you would act accordingly to those habits and beliefs.

Now let's take a look at what beliefs are. Think about what you believe. Where did your beliefs come from? We tend to think that our beliefs are the truth. Many of our beliefs are not the truth! A belief is merely a belief. Look closely at the word *belief* and you will see the word *'lie'* in it! Now I am not suggesting that all of your beliefs are lies, however, if you start to examine your beliefs you will see that many of them are just not true! If you repeat a lie long enough, it will become a belief. Technically speaking, a belief is nothing more than a set of thoughts or ideas which have been impressed upon your brain's neural pathways by being repeated over and over and over and over and over and over again! Beliefs are changing all the time.

The famous scientist Galileo, who Einstein called, 'the father of modern physics' was sentenced to life imprisonment on the basis that he was 'vehemently suspected of heresy' by the church at that time. Galileo stated that the Earth revolved around the Sun rather than the church's view, that Earth was the centre and that the Sun revolved around it. We now know that Galileo was correct. It was not too long ago that we believed that the world was flat! Our five senses can fool us.

I would like to share a personal belief of mine that changed. On July 25, 1978, Louise Brown was born. Louise Brown is the first test tube baby to be born. When I heard about this, I was strongly against it. My thoughts and beliefs were, "Who do they think they are, trying to play God? This is unethical and they have crossed the line!" Now fast forward 20 years to 1998, as I mentioned in the beginning that I have beautiful twin daughters. Well, guess what? They are test tube babies! Do you think my beliefs changed? You see my friends, beliefs are changing all the time. What are some of your limiting beliefs? Take an honest look at what you believe about yourself and others. "I'm not educated enough," or "I can't do that," or "Those people are so bad," or "If you want to be saved, follow us." The list goes on and on.

A belief is not an idea that is held in the mind, it is an idea that holds the mind

So, who are you? You are not the roles you play in life, you are not your body, you are not your thoughts or your beliefs either. You are truly formless. Most people believe that we are human beings, who occasionally have a spiritual experience, when the truth of the matter is that we are spiritual beings having a human experience. When I first heard this statement, it completely altered my world. For the first time, I became aware of my true nature. If I am a spiritual being having a human experience, then I must have existed prior to this physical experience. I came from NO WHERE to NOW HERE and will eventually go back to NO WHERE. All the same letters, just a shift in consciousness. We are always connected to our source. Now you can call this source God, Allah, Krishna, Consciousness, Universe, Infinite Intelligence, or any other 'label' that resonates with you. It is not what you call it. I will use Divine Intelligence to address this source. Think about this, the Divine Intelligence that created the Universe with all of the billions of galaxies, stars, and planets, also created you. I had just briefly mentioned some of the wonders of your body earlier, with all of the amazing functions that take place at lightning speed. All of this symphony of synchronicity is happening without any effort on your part. When you start to get an understanding of this, your whole world changes. The miracle is you! We have access to this Divine Intelligence which is infused in every cell of our being, and in everything, and in every nothing! It is the space between the notes that makes the music. It permeates in the gentle warmth of the sunshine, in the rhythm of the ocean, in the laughter of a child and in the beating of your heart. We are the **Divine Intelligence** manifested. We are a reflection of the Divine Intelligence, which is all there is.

We have the power within us to create because we are of the creator. It is our own thinking, beliefs, and programming that create the experiences we have. So, if it is our own doing, can we change our life experience? Absolutely! When you understand that you create it all and take 100% responsibility for it, you are free. You are no longer the victim of circumstances and now with this awareness, you can reclaim your power. Once you align yourself in harmony with your source, you are in the flow of unlimited potential and in the place of creation. We have access to this in every moment of our lives. The issue is that we have gotten lost in our heads with all the chatter and habitual, self-limiting thoughts that do not serve us.

Start to make an inventory of your most prominent thoughts, and you will quickly see how they show up in your life. When you start to pay attention to your thoughts, at first you will be overwhelmed with the constant chatter and you may even try to stop it. You can't! What you want to do is simply just observe your thoughts and, (this is very important) do not judge them. Just become the silent observer. Do this regularly and you will get very good at detaching yourself from your thoughts. This is called **awareness**.

Now, when it comes to creating your new life experiences, one of the most important questions that you can ask yourself is, "What do I truly want and desire?" Ask yourself this question and really think deeply about it. What do you love to do? What would you do if you could do it seven days a week and it would put a smile on your face? How do you want to serve and make a difference in the world? What have you come here to do? What resonates in your heart? Most people have not spent much time thinking about these things. Even if you have thought about it, most likely you have dismissed it because you cannot see how it will happen, or it seems like a fairy tale.

Did you know that every single person who has ever created anything big or has made incredible discoveries, did not know how they were going to do it in the beginning? All they knew was that they were going to do it! These are the true visionaries of the world. Visioneering is in the realm of the imagination. What is your chief aim in life? Write it down so that you can see it not only on paper but in your imagination. Create a strong mental picture of it and get emotionally attached to it. Your subconscious mind or your emotional mind cannot distinguish if it is imagined or if it is real.

Your thoughts create a mental picture in your mind, then based on what you decide that image 'means' to you, this triggers an emotional response that is expressed through your feelings, which is picked up by the body and then you act upon it. It all starts with your thoughts! Your thoughts manifest in the physical world.

Let me show you how quickly this happens. I'd like you to imagine yourself in the desert. In every direction as far as you can see, all you see is the desert. You are walking alone and you can feel the intense heat radiating from the sand. The sun is beating down on you and the back of your neck is burning. You are perspiring and you feel the salty sweat running down your parched, cracked lips. There is no shade in sight and you feel the heat with every breath that you take as it hits your lungs. You squint to keep the bright sunshine and the sand away from your burning eyes. You see the heat radiating off of the scorching sand. Your body is craving water. The cool, refreshing, sweet comfort of water!

Now let me ask you, are you feeling thirsty? Are you craving water? Is your mouth dry? It most certainly is if you truly imagined it even for a few short minutes! Now let me ask you, were you really in the desert? You created a physical response to an imagined scenario! This is a powerful realization. You only spent a few short minutes imagining this and you had an immediate physical response.

Think about what has been happening in your physical world with your thoughts that you have been repeating for years! How has that showed up in your life? How has that showed up in your body? How has that showed up in your relationships? Here is the good news, you can choose at any moment to change your thoughts to create the life experiences that you desire! We have complete free will. Remember, you come from the source of all creation. You are the artist, you are the painter, you are the choreographer of your life.

We have been given so much freedom and power that we can choose bondage.

For many of us, we do not feel that we are worthy or capable of **greatness**. Where does this come from? It all starts with our programming. Very early on in our lives, we have heard things like "this is the way it is" or "no you can't do that", "how come he/she got better marks than you?", "who do you think you are?", "you will never amount to anything", "stay within your limits", "play it safe", "that's too risky," "we don't do that in our culture or tradition", "why bother, no one loves me anyway." I could go on and on. We all have our versions of these types of comments that completely makes us believe that we are not worthy or great.

According to a UCLA survey, the average one-year-old child hears the word 'no' more than **400** times a day! This becomes our normal way of being and we begin to internalize these feelings of unworthiness and limitation. We have forgotten where we come from. You are worthy! Your very essence is sacred and whole and complete.

When you realize that the 'God' presence resides in you, and in everyone else, you will have a new sense of respect for others and yourself. This presence is what unites us all, as we are all collectively of the one infinite mind. Learn to love yourself from this perspective and you will begin to know how magnificent you truly are!

This is not some feel good jargon, this is the true nature of your being. Love yourself completely and unconditionally. You cannot give something that you yourself do not have. Fill yourself with love, forgiveness, compassion, and gratitude so that you overflow with all of that.

Enlightenment is a destructive process. It is the gentle peeling away of the untruths to reveal your true magnificence.

One of the best ways that I know to get yourself in a state of love and compassion, is to start every day with gratitude. Be grateful for everything! Be grateful that you have eyes to read this, be grateful for the clean drinking water that you have right at your fingertips, be grateful for a hot shower, be grateful for electricity, your bed, clean sheets and pillow, a roof over your head, your health, money, food, for every breath you take. You see, the list is endless! Do this practice every day by writing down ten things that you are grateful for, for the next 60 days and see how things will begin to change. The more grateful you are, the more things will come into your life to be grateful for. I often tell people to be so grateful, that you are ashamed to complain. When you are in a state of **grati-**

tude, you are open to receive more abundance, more good health, more peace and more joy.

We are here for a relatively short period of time. No one knows how much time we have. Our lives are over in just a blink of an eye. Spend your days in gratitude and you will begin to spend your days in a state of heaven.

Life is not happening to you, it is responding to you.

You truly are the creator of your life experience. Understand this and know this intimately. Then begin to design your life the way that you truly desire it to be. Let go of your limiting beliefs and let your imagination free to soar to the highest, most amazing version of you! Remember, your spiritual DNA is perfect. You are sacred and worthy. You are Divine Intelligence manifested. You are here for a flicker in time having a human experience.

I started by talking about my father's dream for his family and I would like to end with a story about my father. After my mother passed away six years ago, my father was adamant about living on his own. We respected his wishes for as long as we could. I am so blessed to have such loving and caring siblings as we all took the time to care for him. It became apparent to me one day that he could no longer be on his own, when I walked into his apartment to find him in bed shivering with fear and curled up like a little child, so afraid to even look out from under the covers. He would stay in bed all day by himself.

My father was a very proud and disciplined man, who never wanted to feel like a burden on anyone. He had been very clear on his desire to be independent, however on this day I had decided that he would come and live with me. When I said to him "I'm taking you home with me" he did not resist at all. At that point, I knew in my heart that he had surrendered to his yearning for love.

I consider it a great blessing and honour that we were able to care for our parents as a family. This taught us all a great lesson on love, compassion, and forgiveness. We cared for him for a few more years and we shared many stories about his life, his dreams, his regrets and his life-long pain of growing up without his parents who had died when he was very young. Then his health began to deteriorate quite rapidly where he became bedridden. Once again, I saw in his eyes his sadness of being helpless. I began to care for him 24 hours a day and making him as comfortable as possible.

I could see that he was slipping away and on December 10, 2014, I expressed my thoughts in a message sent to family and friends which I would like to share with you.

As I watch the flame of life slowly fading away in my father, I began to reflect on his life and all of the buried treasures of wisdom and lessons. On a few occasions he has expressed his regret for not doing certain things in his life. I see the pain of "I should have" in his eyes. "If only I would have done…"

This has re-ignited in me the desire to express myself in alignment with my purpose in life. What is your reason for being here? What is your gift to the world? Begin to listen to your heart and allow the Divine Intelligence to guide you. You will know when you are living your life in alignment be-cause you will feel more alive than you ever have. You will lose track of time and will have so much more energy. It is only our limiting beliefs that stop us. Would it not be a be-

trayal of the Divine to not use the gifts and talents given to us? Every breath you take is an affirmation of the God force within all of us affirming "You are alive!" How can we ignore this gift? We have available within us unlimited potential. You are here to express your gifts and you will not feel complete until you do.

Thank you, father, for teaching me everything that you have taught me. Through the pain and the joy, it is the whole that makes up the tapestry of our life experience.

Give thanks for all of the teachers and loved ones that have come into your lives. They all had gifts for you! Especially the ones that push your buttons! Take a moment to send them your love and appreciation. Your expression of love will transcend this realm and vibrate out to all of them, wherever they are. As it has been said, "Don't die with your music still in you" for it is only a matter of time when your flame of life will flicker and fade away. Open your heart as every moment is a gift, every breath you take is a gift. Life is a gift and gifts are meant to be opened.

On Friday, December 12, 2014, as I sat by my father's side holding his hand, I felt his body releasing and his spirit returning back home. He passed away gently in the early afternoon.

As I end this journey with you here now, I direct you back full circle to the beginning quote and remind you that you are a spiritual being having a human experience. Live your life to the fullest and open your unique gift to share with the world.

*"In Reality, you are so much more than you think
you are...
In your Reality, you are no more than you think
you are."*

Mahmood Sheikh is the President of Powermind Corporation. A company dedicated to multiplying the growth and productivity of both individuals and companies for maximum results.

His specialized training enables him to empower and educate others on, "How To Think Effectively" to achieve their desired result. Powermind Corporation also offers workshops teaching the application of stock market techniques and strategies, assisting individuals to achieve early financial freedom.

Mahmood Sheikh is a Keynote speaker, co-author, mentor and coach. He's acquired many years of study on the subjects of co-creating your life and personal development.

For more information please contact mahmoods@powermind.ca

11

HOW DO YOU WANT TO FINISH?

By Wayne Kuhn

"You are never too old to set another goal or dream a new dream."

C.S. LEWIS

It's Thursday morning and I am on my way to William's Café for a coffee and perhaps, a forbidden muffin that tastes so good. Every Thursday morning the men from our church, who are mostly retired, meet for coffee at 9:00am sharp. The group varies in numbers from 15 to 20 men ranging from 60 to 90 years of age. Needless to say, I am one of the youngest attending.

They chat about lots of different topics such as what trips they took in the last few months, what the grandchildren are up to, what surgeries are going on and occasionally, who died that week. As I look around the group, I see Fred at 86, Ken at 85 and Bill at 83, all very active, sharp of mind and full of stories and life experiences.

My thoughts drift off as I do some math. I take their age and subtract mine. **WOW!** The result is exciting. I'm filled with hope. I have more than 20 years of life before catching up to most of them. I have 20 years to pursue my lifelong dream!

I like to join these fellows whenever possible as I find their conversations interesting and inspiring. I am usually one of the first to leave as I have appointments to attend. Sometimes as I leave, they joke, "You better go sell another house to make sure we get our pension cheques." I laugh inside. I know most of them are retired professors, engineers and entrepreneurs who have so much money, they don't need their pension cheques. I leave William's with a spring in my step and a smile on my face. I'm excited about the future, excited about my dream and feeling good about the decisions I have made.

Let me fill you in on what has happened in my life. As a real estate broker I have it all, a vehicle and and profession that can take me anywhere. Yes, I love the profession of real estate and have done it for 30 years. But, was I ready to coast to the finish line? Was this the way I wanted to finish?

When you are comfortable and life is too easy, there is a tendency to sit back and coast. However, if you have ever watched something that is coasting, it must be going downhill or it won't move. You never coast up a hill.

Knowing I had many years ahead, I often wondered if this was all there was to life. Was this as good as it gets for me? At the age of 63, I saw many people my age retiring from jobs and careers where they had put in 30 to 40 years of dedicated time and energy with one focus in mind. To retire. And then what? Sit at home with no direction, no hopes, no dreams, just coasting and then, they die a young death?

Did I want to be one of those people who coasted toward the finish line, waiting to die? It sounded profound and quite sad, but was it real? The phrase, **"How do I want to finish?"** repeated over and over in my mind. I loved real estate. There was nothing else I wanted to do... or was there?

Ever since the late 1980's, while attending many MLM (multi-level marketing) conferences, I would see motivational speakers on stage charging up the audience. I had this feeling, a deep-down desire, a vision that someday I would stand on stage in front of thousands of people and share my message. Whatever that would be, I didn't know at the time.

In 1993 I joined a Toastmaster club because I wanted to be like Tony Robbins. I climbed the ranks in Toastmasters to become a DTM (Distinguished Toastmaster), the highest level one can reach in Toastmasters. I also entered many speaking contests and won at many levels. But, I still wasn't Tony Robbins on a stage speaking to thousands of people. Was this a fantasy that I would take to my grave?

Was it a dream that would never come true? Was it a dream that would eventually fade as I coasted closer to the finish line? Or could I actually revive and "recharge" my dream of becoming an International Professional Speaker and travel the world inspiring those I meet?

Could I RECHARGE, put the "**throttle down**" and give it all I could, so that when I did cross that finish line, I would know and the world would know that I gave it my best? That I gave it my ALL? But first, I had to ask myself an important question. Was I willing to make the changes necessary to become the person I wanted to be? Change was no stranger to me. In the past, I'd made two major changes in my life.

In 1987 I left the security of a regular pay cheque and a 15 year employment in the electronic industry. I ventured out into the wilds of commission sales where one month you'd be rich from the results of many sales and the next month you'd be poor as a result of too few or no sales. However, I was in control.

I was familiar with the risks and rewards of being an entrepreneur. Having some exposure to MLM (multi-level marketing) on a part time basis, I knew what I wanted. I chose Real Estate for three reasons. I wanted:

1. A product that people loved and needed.
2. The ability to earn as much as I wanted.
3. To work as much as I wanted or as little as I wanted. My time would be my own.

At the age of 50, I made the second major change in my life. I walked away from a 30 year marriage because I didn't see any hope. I knew that I didn't want the next 30 years of my life to be like my last 30. Having gone through the stress and complications of separation, divorce and a career change, I knew I could handle another major change if I needed to.

After a friend introduced me to the book *"Think And Grow Rich"* by Napoleon Hill, my thoughts of the future started to change. The book talks about how our thoughts and feelings dramatically affect our results. It describes how we all have a paradigm which is a collection of our habits. We can change this paradigm if we create different habits which gives us different results. If this were true, then which of my thoughts were holding me back from following my dream? One of Napoleon Hill's quotes that struck me was:

"Whatever the mind of man can conceive and believe, it can achieve."

Sound a bit far-fetched? I contemplated giving it a try. What if I revitalized my dream and wrote it out every day? What if I visualized it and started working every day, step by step towards it? Why not? What did I have to lose?

I became a successful Realtor when the odds were highly against me. I made other significant changes in my life that at the time I thought I could never survive. And with my 24 years of Toastmaster experience, I was quite comfortable as a speaker/presenter on stage.

The only thing holding me back was what was between my ears: my thoughts and beliefs. The what if's. So, I took action. I visualized what I wanted. I became excited and emotional about what I wanted. Every day I repeated it out loud. I started writing out this affirmation: "I am so happy and grateful that I am now an International Professional Speaker and I fly all over the world speaking to thousands of people. I inspire others to RE/CHARGE... to get excited about their dreams."

I wrote it on a card and carried it with me all the time, reading it with passion and excitement every chance I had.

I started to connect and surround myself with people who believed in me. People who encouraged me to reach for my dream. People with a dream of their own.

I joined a **mastermind group** that meets every week. We talk about our wins, the things that are going right on our journey. We share what we've learned from our daily reading of material written by authors who inspire, motivate and encourage. I ask for and receive help from the mastermind group, about barriers and obstacles I face as I move closer and closer to my goal.

So what has changed? It's my thinking that has changed. Becoming a professional speaker used to be just a fantasy. It was something sitting in the back of my mind which I thought would never become reality.

Now, every day I move closer to my goal of being a professional speaker. Some days are better than others, however, keeping a regular routine of focusing on my goal helps me a lot. I take every opportunity to speak and inspire others about how they, too, can make their dream a reality. I connect and interview other people who are striving to become professional speakers so that I can learn from their experiences.

For 30 years Real Estate has been my passion and it will remain an important part of my wealth building strategy. Over the next 20 years I will continue helping people build wealth through real estate but with the new added excitement of teaching them to "recharge" their lives, dream big, dust off their fantasies and be the person they want to be.

Oh, guess what? Now, it's Thursday morning and I'm on my way to "Williams Café" for a coffee and maybe a muffin, and to hear from the guys about what happened this week. I continue my visits with them as often as I can and also to share my journey with them. I know some day when I am 90 years old and some young fellow in his 60's joins the group and is thinking about retiring, I can ask him, "How do you want to finish? Have you done everything you want to do in life? What unfulfilled dreams and fantasies are inside you? How can I help you make your dreams come true?"

How do you want to finish?

Wayne Kuhn is from Kitchener, Ontario and is married to Suzanne Saunders. Together they have five adult boys and four busy grandchildren. Wayne has been a real estate broker for 30 years specializing in residential home sales and first time investors who want to build their wealth through real estate.

Wayne has been a member of the Black Walnut Toastmaster Club since 1993. In 2008 Wayne earned his DTM (Distinguished

Toastmaster) designation, the highest designation possible through Toastmasters International. Toastmasters is an organization dedicated to the improvement of communication and leadership skills.

Having won many awards for speaking, Wayne loves facilitating workshops and conducting seminars relating to real estate and personal development. Wayne is enthusiastic about life and brings this energy and passion for life to everyone he meets. If you wish to contact Wayne, you can reach out to him at wayne@waynekuhn.com

12

BLUE AMBER

By Sonal Raje

"Let the rays of creative inspiration reveal the beauty within"

SONAL RAJE

December 2013: Annual show of the Société Nationale des Beaux-Arts at The Louvre in Paris.

On a dark wall there is a painting, "Thin Ice." The artist has captured the precarious surface of a lake about to be covered with a thin sheet of ice. The evergreens lining the lake cast shadows on the ice and reflections in water. The painting holds the gaze of art lovers taking in the vast talent displayed in this prestigious show in the art capital of the world. Awards are announced, and "Thin Ice" gets a bronze medal. The applause fills the room and the artist's heart.

December 2015: Canada

I wake up in a sweat in the middle of a frigid December night at home in Canada. I walk down the steps quietly to my studio and close my palms around the medal. The cold metal is comforting. I look around my studio, at the untouched brushes and paints on the shelves, blank canvases lined against the wall. "Thin Ice" stares at me from across the room. I can feel the beseeching gaze. Someday, I promise quietly, not just yet, when I am on more solid ground. I had been saying that for the past two years.

Yes, you guessed right. I am Sonal Raje, Canadian artist, and member of the 2013 Canadian delegation to Paris. And yes again, I had stopped painting after that show. Why, you ask? I was serving a sentence. I had banished the artist within me to a world where there were no colours. My heart was filled with deep sorrow. I had lost my father just before the show in Paris. We had immigrated to Canada 10 years back, and could only visit my family in India once every couple of years. I would talk to my dad on Sundays and his first words always felt like a warm hug: "From Canada with Love."

Life was busy with my growing children and our new careers. We saw wonderful opportunities in this beautiful and welcoming country. Just as we were living with a sense of gratitude with all that we had achieved, I got the news of my father's failing health. I rushed to India, and met him for the last time for just a couple of days. I was shocked to see his frail body, and he was breathing his last few breaths. In the next moment he was gone. I had no idea of the pain and suffering he had gone through. He did not reach out for us as we were too far, and busy with making a life for ourselves in a new country. The tragedy of death was followed by unfortunate family disputes, that tore the rest of the family apart. I came home to my own family in Canada with a heavy heart. I literally dragged myself to the show in Paris a few months later.

Everything after that is a haze of grey mist, black shadows and dim lights. I lost touch with myself. Outwardly my life seemed perfect, the mother and wife within me were on autopilot. I had turned the regret I felt as a daughter into blame on my artist self for being self absorbed, and shut out the colours. The dis-ease in my mind manifested as disease of the body and ended up in a series of health problems. Yet I could not will myself to make the effort to open up to a little light in my heart.

I had realized I was hurting myself and my family by this isolation, and one fateful Tuesday evening, I accompanied some friends to a motivational talk. In that bright room, I felt like I had entered a world that I had left behind for too long. All around were happy, hopeful, kind faces, and inspiring, empowering words like goals, change, results, focus, achievement, swirled around my senses. I was drawn into the powerful energy, which encompassed my soul. As I closed my eyes, I felt the loving hug of my father and heard the words, "You are in the right place, accept this gift... From Canada with Love." And so I did, this wonderful blessing that gave me the will and strength to take a leap of faith and lead myself back to the place that I had abandoned.

I was given a chance to re-invent myself with awareness and informed decisions. At times we all need some direction and discipline if we want to change the way we are shaping our life. Knowing that you are not alone can be the first step towards gathering courage to embark on the journey of empowerment. If we can break through our limiting beliefs and fears that hold us back, we can realize our potential and not be a victim of circumstance. It is certain that time helps to heal the hurt, dissipate the anger and blunt the pain, but only if we can find it within ourselves to understand, accept and forgive the past with compassion. For this we need to be in a place of mindful awareness. I opened my eyes to a new reality, was living in the present again and looking towards the future.

The Blue Amber is a rare gemstone found in the Caribbean island of Dominican Republic. Under the rays of sunlight, its earthy amber colour magically changes to a brilliant turquoise of the ocean. I found this magical place in my heart that shines with a new light under the rays of divine inspiration on this path towards finding and fulfilling my life purpose. I am ready to reveal my true self. I chose to live authentically instead of role playing. And I am not alone. I walk alongside a supportive and inspiring community of friends and mentors. Together we strive to better ourselves.

December 2016:

My studio is filled with bustle, excitement and chatter of the universal language of Art as I share my processes with my groups. There is a magnificent disarray of paints and brushes all around, and the colourful canvases smile on the walls. My new painting "Mirage" is displayed at The Louvre in Paris in the 2016 show. My heart fills with gratitude to have been guided on this path, and is humbled by the lessons that life has taught.

Today, I am filled with a sense of peace and purpose. Every person holds within himself or herself a special gift.

What we do with that gift defines our role within the community that nurtures us. I have used my art to heal, discover, and express myself. I continue to do so, but not in isolation anymore. I am inspired to share and spread the power of intuitive and expressive art practices with the community that has accepted me with love and support. I have studied and practice holistic approaches that heal and nurture the body and soul.

As I move ahead, I have had to make some painful decisions of letting go of some attachments that were once very dear, but could not accompany me anymore. Though short-lived, every experience is part of a whole that continues to shape us as a person. Once we release these attachments with love, we make a place for infinite possibilities to fill up the space.

Opening up to the light has put me back in touch with all the seven colours contained in every ray of light. I see colour with the eyes of my soul, as the energy that flows through our bodies, and also reflected around us in nature.

We all are a precious Blue Amber, waiting for the rays of light to shine upon us, and the source of that light is within each of our beautiful souls.

> *"You have given me back the forgotten and*
> *the true. Blessed anew, the Amber shines Blue"*

SONAL RAJE

Sonal Raje is a professional artist based in Guelph, Canada. Her paintings express emotions through the use of colour, form and texture. Her cultural roots in India, travels through Europe, and the natural beauty of her hometown Guelph have all contributed towards this process. Her art has been shown and acclaimed at shows in Toronto, New York, Florence, Budapest, Mumbai and Paris. Her art was chosen among the Canadian delegation at the annual show of "Fine Arts Society of Paris" at The Louvre in Paris. She received a Bronze medal at this show from the "Arts, Sciences and Lettres" society of France.

Her paintings are available on her website, and at local art galleries. She also has a line of silk scarves with prints of her original artwork. Her vision is to promote expressive arts as a language of self-discovery and exploration. She volunteers at the Art Therapy programs at the Hospice in Guelph. She does energy work as a certified Reiki healer, Angel card reader and Therapeutic Touch practitioner. She incorporates these intuitive processes in her Expressive Arts programs for the community in Meetup groups, at seniors' residences and for the special needs community. These programs can also be accessed as online modules.

Sonal Raje
www.blueamberarts.com
blueamberarts@gmail.com

13

YOUR INTERNAL GIFTS
By Claudette Snow

"A treasure chest of wisdom floats within your soul. When utilized correctly the reward is wealth, in all aspects of life."

CLAUDETTE SNOW

There are so very many things in life that we never give any true consideration. Things that matter and can make a tremendous impact on every outcome of every situation. The majority of people seem to conform to the masses. In other words, they follow the crowd. I often wonder if it's pure ignorance or if it's just easier to be like everyone else. Perhaps it's both. I know for myself, that was the case.

I'd spent the majority of my life following the crowd, doing exactly what was expected of me by other people. Growing up in a blue-collar family meant that I would follow in the paths of those before me. That's what I saw, that's how I was programmed. It wasn't that I didn't have dreams or fantasize about living in a castle, because I did. I just never shared my dreams. I kept them locked safely away in the walls of my **imagination**. I would lay awake at night picturing myself as a lawyer, doctor, model or even a writer.

Those visions were quickly banished from my mind as I heard the tired voices of my parents in the predawn hours, leaving for their factory jobs. My parents worked hard and long to provide for our family. We always had clean clothes and home cooked meals. We were loved and we knew it. They sacrificed many things for themselves to provide for four girls. We often wore milk bags over our socks before slipping on our winter boots. Layering up three or four pairs of mismatched mittens in winter wasn't uncommon and if you owned a second vehicle, you were considered wealthy.

I wish I'd been able to go through childhood as a sound sleeper, but that wasn't the case. I'd heard many conversations and discussions of heartache. Life was a continuous struggle and it made me angry. Why were the two most important people in my life having to give up so much for everyone else? They were smart, funny and wonderful yet, I vowed never to be like them.

As the years drifted by, my dreams and fantasies became dimmer with the environment and friends I had surrounding me. **I no longer used my imagination** to conjure up visions of the way I wanted my life to be. I just seemed to fall in line with those around me, did whatever they were doing.

That worked pretty well during elementary school. I'd only had one friend and she kept me well entertained. I'd come to accept what most of the other girls said, "We'll grow up someday, get married and have babies of our own." I'd watch them jump up and down and squeal like they'd just won the lottery. I'd jumped right along with them, the whole time thinking, "Why in heavens would they want to do that?" Somewhere in the back of my mind, I had different ideas about being happy. I just didn't know what they were yet.

Just before seventh grade, my family packed and moved away to the other side of town. We had a new home and many adjustments to make. For me, the biggest adjustment was learning how to fit in. I'd carried my childhood innocence with me from the old neighbourhood to the new. I'd realized rather quickly that I wasn't going to fit in very well in my new modern environment.

Our house was bigger and better, I got my own room, no more sharing. My parents were happy and things seemed fantastic... sort of. My mom didn't have to walk 30 minutes to work, she now got to ride a bus. That seemed rather exciting, not worth expressing how miserable I was.

From my early teen years, friends were all that mattered. I have two older siblings and one younger. They all seemed to adapt quite well. What was wrong with me?

I was miserable, made fun of on a daily basis for one thing or another. I was taunted and teased and would hunt for any detour possible on my way home, to avoid running into those who made my life difficult. Most days I failed. I kept wondering what was wrong with these kids. I never understood their mentality, aggression or negative mindsets.

Eventually, I was accepted into a small group of girls. They were popular, wild, loud and obnoxious. They were pure trouble and that's exactly how I spent the majority of my teenage years, being in big trouble.

Whatever was suggested, I went along with. It didn't matter how stupid, dangerous or crazy. I had a lump in my throat and a pain in my stomach every time we hung out, knowing things seldom ended well. I was either in trouble at school or trouble at home. More times than not, I was in trouble at both. I knew I didn't feel comfortable or fit in with this group but if I wanted to have friends, I had to pretend to be like them, or so I thought. I didn't like them and I didn't like myself for being with them. Not once did it occur to me that **I had a choice**. Having the wrong friends seemed better than having none at all.

I was grateful for having my own money from babysitting jobs and later acquiring a part time sales position at the local mall. By fifteen, I slowly started to witness the difference between myself and my so-called friends. I was excited to share my news of landing my first real job. They were anything but happy for me. They couldn't comprehend why I'd want go to work and I couldn't understand why they didn't.

I enjoyed going to my job, working with people, collecting a paycheque I knew I'd earned. I often took the bus to and from work. There were many occasions when these girls were waiting to greet me from my bus ride home. Initially, they said I was missed, and wanted to hang out. I was far too tired, had school in the morning and needed to sleep. My response was met with cruel insults and nasty name calling. I'd walked home without incident. Several visits later, I wasn't so lucky. As I'd stepped from the bus, three of them were waiting. It wasn't hard to see they were hopped up on something.

I stood no chance at slipping away unnoticed and they quickly grabbed me by the arms and snatched my purse. While two held me in place, the other riffled through my things. Rewarded with my last five dollars, she dumped the remaining contents and with her boots, ground everything like sawdust into the dirt. Noticing a woman watching through her window, they shoved me to the pavement, laughing hysterically while making their getaway.

While I was hurt both physically and emotionally, I somehow was not surprised by this encounter. Everything my younger self had tried to warn me about had finally hit home. That lump in my throat, the upset stomach, the feeling of not fitting in, was my own built in warning mechanism. That is called my **intuition** and I wish I'd recognized it sooner.

The message here is, **always follow your gut instincts**. If you feel something is wrong or not right, listen to that feeling. It will never lead you down the wrong path. My youth and inexperience had blocked my **awareness** and left me in a state of ignorance. I have become a master at following my instincts from that day forward.

I continued to work part-time in sales while going to classes. I struggled to receive passing grades in most courses. Creative writing was the only area I truly excelled in and enjoyed. I couldn't wait for high school to end.

Before completing my final year, an opportunity came my way. The biggest, highest-paying factory in town was hiring. My whole family worked there and I knew I'd be accepted if I applied. I felt guilty even thinking about it. I remembered the many times I'd told my mom, "I will never work in a factory." She'd always reply with a simple, "Good, I hope you won't have to".

But you know what happened, don't you? I applied, got accepted and went to work for what was considered to be the best family owned company in Canada, J.M. Schneider Inc. I was young, single and considered financially blessed. I didn't have a care in the world. I bought whatever I wanted, whenever I wanted. I had nice clothes, nice vehicles and worked as many weekends as possible to have even more. I was so **grateful** for my health and wealth. I had met the best people I'd ever known. I planned on working there until I could retire.

Those childhood dreams had completely vanished from my mind, I was living my new reality. I was driven. I'd built a business and sold it. I'd bought a home. I'd worked hard, as much and as often as possible, often taking college courses on the side as well as second jobs. I couldn't imagine life being any better.

That's usually when your wakeup call comes, mine was no different. It arrived in the form of bone cancer when I was 32 and riding the wave of my life. It was very aggressive and spreading rapidly. I needed to handle the situation as quickly as possible and get back to living. That was my plan, until I'd experienced a drug-induced heart attack on the operating table, due to an error made by the anesthesiologist.

Was I upset? "No," not really. Disappointed perhaps? "Yes." We are all capable of errors and mistakes, and we are all worthy of **forgiveness**. I was given a heartfelt apology and that was good enough for me. I had things to do. Shortly after being discharged from the hospital, I'd heard rumours of downsizing at the company I worked for. Oddly enough, this news was more devastating to me than the cancer diagnosis. It turned out to be true. I was going to lose the very job I'd said I would never do, but did and loved.

Sixteen and a half years of luxury were being erased from my life, which meant I would lose everything that came with it. And I did. Goodbye to the health benefits and paid vacations, no more large hourly wage or company picnics. What would I do now? I had plenty of time to think about it. I had a bandaged hip from bone grafting, a cast on my arm, crutches to walk and an order to have cardiac strengthening.

During this time of difficulty and loss, I had no direction and absolutely no clue what was going to happen to me. Apparently, that was only my **perception** because the Universe had a plan of its own, and presented me with an unexpected gift. He was tall, dark and handsome. I used my **reasoning** faculty to determine there had to be something incredibly wrong with this man. Surely he was desperate. After all, I had cancer… no employment, no income and nothing left to offer. He decided to use his will and prove to me that **life isn't about what you can get from others, but more about what you have to offer**. Once again, I was counting on my **intuition** to guide me in the right direction and it did.

He stayed true to his word and saw me through every hospital visit and treatment. We never stopped believing in the outcome we had wanted. Being told that childbirth was unlikely, we left it in the hands of the Universe. Nine months from our wedding night, our miracle child was born. We never doubted for a minute. **We asked, we believed, we received**. That's the way it works.

We are all brought into the world with many gifts in the form of **intellectual faculties**. It is our duty to develop them to ensure a glorious life. I look back within my memory on my earlier, younger life and remember the lessons taught to me the hard way. They showed me I have value, they've proved to me I count. They've added so much height to my awareness.

The greatest lesson I could share with others is to never, ever follow the crowd. Do not conform from fear of standing alone. It is you and only you who has to live your life. It is your individuality that sets you apart and makes you special and unique. Cherish the relationship you have with yourself and know that it will be the most important relationship you will ever have.

Marriage and parenting brought along a new set of challenges. Things happened along the way, I never saw coming and had no way of preparing for. I needed to re-evaluate who I was and what I wanted from my life. Again, I had to acknowledge that I'd fallen into a trap of conformity. I was a wife, a mother, a homemaker.

I hadn't been in the workforce forever. I had spent the last 20 years doing what I thought was expected of me. I was cooking, cleaning, and making sure everyone else was happy. I became a drone while everyone around me was moving up and moving on. I had no clue who I was. I had become nothing more than the wallpaper that surrounded them. I was invisible. I took this as a sign from a higher power. I had to really dig deep, know what I wanted and go after it.

As I sat quietly alone, trying to understand what was happening in my life, I closed my eyes and every childhood fantasy came reeling back to me. I compared those dreams to what I still wanted. The one that screamed loud and clear was, "I'm going to be a writer." I made the decision to pursue the one message that was constant throughout my life. It was difficult to accept and even harder to believe. "Could I be the somebody who might make a difference with the words I put on paper?"

Believing in myself was not something I was used to, but connecting the dots looking back gave me a reason to accept that maybe... just maybe, I could do this. I am not my parents, I am not my friends but more importantly, I am not my past. I am me. I am special. I am an individual who has followed her gut, her heart and her mind. I followed my **intuition**.

I'd waited many years ignoring what I'd always wanted to be. The signs kept pointing me in the right direction but I always chose the opposite. I'd never accepted that I could actually do, exactly what I truly wanted to do. It seemed too unreal, too magical. Then I took a good, long look in the mirror and said, "Why not? You are just as good as anybody else. What do you have to lose by trying?"

I knew from past experience that it was so important, to listen to my inner voice, the signs laid before me and the opportunities that continued to appear.

Although I was approaching midlife, I had to take the leap and follow my instincts. It's been a very rewarding journey. Dreams really do come true and it's never too late to do what you always knew you'd wanted to. **Ask, Believe and Receive**. That's the way it works.

14

SECOND CHANCE

By Mirella L. Muise

Ever since I was a little girl I had the desire to be above the ordinary. It was **fear** that I wouldn't be noticed, one of the many children lost in an ocean of humanity.

"If you are looking for the secret to knowing how to be the best that you can be, start reading. The secret of the ages is hidden in books" my dad said. I must have been in grade one or two because reading at that age was still new and slow but there was my answer, I had to read. As a teenager, I would find reasons not to go out with my friends. Their idea of fun was to party and drink, mine was to go to the library.

My city, big and busy, is called Timisoara and is in Romania. The public library is a turn of the century building, filled with millions of books. The structure, designed as a large square, encompassed an open area, filled with comfortable benches to sit while reading under one of the many trees planted there. Summertime was absolutely beautiful, surrounded by nature, a good book, feeling the warm sun's rays on my body and listening to the birds sing.

Even now when life gets hard and hectic I recall the memory, the way it felt. I close my eyes and I am there, with some old book. The cover is hard and used. I can smell the pages of pure happiness and I disappear into the world of whatever book I am reading. This is my happy place. I guess it's accurate to say that I wasn't, "street smart." I was living in my own imaginary world of books and believed people were good and honest. I still believe that and most of the time it's true.

I said "yes," to a new guy I'd met who wanted to marry me. At 18, I'd thought I had a pretty good understanding of what I wanted. At that time, my country was still under the communist regime. The people started to talk about wanting to do something to change the oppressive communist party. "Freedom," this was the word and the concept that we all dreamed about. We were tired of the oppression, lack of everything, the unfairness and corruption.

We, the people had to do something to make changes. I remember praying for my country and praying for strength to make it possible. The day before the revolution started I remember going home to my husband, it was December 1989. I'd just found out that we were going to have a baby. My heart was beating rapidly and I felt horrific fear engulfing me as if a cloud had swallowed me whole. I didn't know exactly what was going to happen, but I knew it was important and I wanted to be a part of if. The next day I went to the city centre with lots of other people, I was only there in the beginning. People started to say, "Down with communism, freedom to all."

With each passing hour, more people started to join our group. The street was now full. The crowds were louder and louder and the police feared riots and disorder. The authorities sent the army to disburse the demonstration and establish order. We were told to leave or else they would use weapons against us. We held hands and started to chant louder, "Down with Communism, freedom to our people!!!" The army started to shoot and I could see bodies falling to the ground. Some of us ran for cover and made makeshift hospitals to look after the wounded… crazy times.

Other cities started to go out to the centre of their city in solidarity of Timisoara. The army refused to continue shooting and hurting the people. The next days were filled with chaos and fear. Everyone knew that we were at the point of no return. We were going to be free or die.

I remember being so happy that my dad was already gone from the country. He'd escaped the year before and was in Austria. If my dad would have been there, he would have been dead. I was convinced he would have been in the front rows, maybe driving one of the military tanks.

My mother and sister followed my dad to Austria not long after the revolution, when the borders finally opened. I was married and couldn't follow them. I had my son in August 1990. With my family gone abroad, I was left to fend for myself. Unfortunately, my marriage didn't last. Knowing there wasn't anything left, I took my son with nothing more than the clothes on our backs and never returned.

My son and I grew up together, we went through hardships, but we stayed strong. We were going to leave Romania to join my family in Canada. They had all immigrated there after a few years in Austria. We are now here in Canada, my son Flavius and I are finally free. For me, it was an opportunity to start new, fresh, make better choices and have a better life. After gaining employment and doing my best, something inside of me would say, "This is not going to last, you don't deserve this, you are not good enough, you are forever destined for mediocrity..."

Within a few years of living in Canada, I met the most wonderful man. He is strong and unafraid to allow me to be as bold as I want. He recognizes my free spirit and loves me without trying to change me in any way. I knew that he possessed rare qualities and felt blessed that he loved me.

I changed my career a few times, always looking for the one thing that would make me happy. I said to myself that I had to find the one thing that I am passionate about, that wouldn't feel like work, something fun. Working for BMW in sales is definitely fun, every day is a different day. I have a purpose, I am making a difference. Wanting to be the best that I can be, giving the best service that I can, has allowed me to be respected and has created a loyal customer base.

In spite of it all, my **outer image** was not in harmony with my **inside image**. I appeared to be a strong, bold woman, successful in a man's world. However, the way I saw myself was as a scared, insecure, little girl that runs and hides. I would be successful, but it was hit and miss. I didn't understand how to constantly make it a successful month. My sales were good sometimes yet not so good at others. I would get ahead, then I would lose some. I would hit this invisible ceiling that I didn't know how to break through. This created a lot of frustration. It was the "**FEAR**" that I wasn't good enough. I wanted to be the greatest sales person but I didn't know how to consistently make it happen, how to plan, how to increase my sales or how to attract new leads on a constant basis.

My life journey came to a complete halt one day, everything got really quiet. November 2014, I was driving myself to the family doctor but didn't make it. I pulled over on the side of the road, called my husband to say goodbye. Today was the day, I was going to die. The ambulance took me to the nearest hospital, the pain in my head was unbelievable and nobody knew how to stop it. They checked me, did all the tests but couldn't understand what was happening. Kevin, (my husband) took me home later that day, even though I couldn't walk anymore. It will be better tomorrow, or not... The next day, it was clear I had experienced a stroke. I'd had only partial vision and lost all ability to walk, drink or eat.

I was sent to Hamilton General Hospital. The days spent in the hospital, were an eye opener to understand the value of being healthy, and how much I took that for granted. I said to myself that I will get back on my feet and I will look for what's important to me. I will learn to be true to myself and never, ever live like I will never die. I will live every day as if it's my last.

After I was released from the hospital I went right back to work. Walking with a cane was good enough for me, at least I was walking. Perhaps this was my wake up call to stop running, stop and think. I went back to books to find my answers.

One day a customer came to the dealership, I was getting ready to leave for home. Everyone was busy so it was up to me to welcome this customer to BMW Grand River. We started to talk and somehow the conversation went away from the purpose of his visit. I'd realized that this person knew things that other people didn't. I was fascinated by the way he was carrying himself, he was confident and calm. It was something that he said that opened a discussion about the power of the mind. After he left the dealership we decided to stay in touch.

This was the beginning, he introduced me to people that were like minded. I started to learn how to **improve on the inside** first, how to understand **who I really am** and what I want from this life. I learned the power of having a goal, to having a direction in life. I learned how to plan every day by using the **power of my mind**, because we are what we think about.

For the longest time, I thought if I just found that one person that could make me happy, then everything would be alright. Every new love in my life was going to be that person. I would be happy now, but every time I was disappointed. How silly it feels now, that race to find the right person almost killed me. Nobody is responsible for my happiness but me and only me.

With the help of my new friends, I am learning how my habits, long time beliefs, and limitations that exist in my mind, have everything to do with the results I see in my life. No more hit and miss success. Now I plan and succeed as sure as day comes after night.

"You have nothing to do with your coming into this world. You may have little or nothing to do with your leaving it. But you have almost everything to do with your life while you possess that life."

NAPOLEON HILL

The image I have of myself is the secret. I am the only one that can change who I am and become the memorable human being that I have aspired to be all my life.

"There are no limitations to the mind except those we acknowledge, both poverty and riches are the offspring of thought."

NAPOLEON HILL

I have finally found peace and love, I actually like the person I've become. I am happy and grateful for the second chance at living life. I have a direction, I have a goal and I know where I want to be. I wake up every morning happy, that today is another day that will take me closer to my goal. It's an amazing way to be.

Mirella lives in Kitchener, Ontario with her husband Kevin. She works at BMW Grand River and is recognized as a top sales representative. If you would like to contact Mirella, she may be reached at mirellapopescu@rogers.com.

15

DROWNING IN SUCCESS

By S. Kirsten Flynn

"There is only one person you have to live with your entire life and that's you. I suggest you like your company because it's a lifetime relationship that you can't get out of."

S. KIRSTEN FLYNN

Have you ever been so high on life that even a pinch couldn't convince you that it wasn't a dream? I have, and I so desperately want that feeling back again.

I've spent years refining my career which is a beautiful collection of sales, operations, management and executive positions. All of which I love, and come with their own individual challenges and rewards. When I finally landed my first Vice President position, I knew that I was one title away from my lifelong desire, "to be the head of a corporation." I would lead with integrity, dignity, and profitability.

Being a natural morning person, I was in the office early and always reviewed my emails before leaving the house. I had my agenda formulated in my mind before I sat at my desk. The first year was no cakewalk. This was a very male dominant industry and women were still mainly viewed as, "Administrative Assistants." I'd excelled in my position and every task assigned was met with great achievement, as I went above and beyond the requirements. The upside was the positive environment I'd created at head office. The downside, my positive productivity seemed to agitate some high level executives, to the point of creating what felt like a hostile environment.

With the restructuring, the intimidating atmosphere was abolished and I'd inherited a mountain of corporate nightmares. Some were small but important, others large and critical. I absolutely loved diving into the mechanics of the corporate machine, pulling it apart, cleaning or replacing the cogs and putting it all back together again. It really was my forte so it never really felt like work.

Life can sure be funny during the high times, it almost blinded me to the obvious events that were shaping up around me. That year, I'd implemented more marketing initiatives, corporate communications and gave the employees a voice. Obviously, I was doing something right because two days after the yearly conference I was contacted by a production company. They wanted to feature me in the television show, "Undercover Boss Canada." Yes! I was floating on cloud nine, tangled in its silver lining, and couldn't believe that I'd finally made it... almost.

I'd made our company an overnight sensation and the envy of our competition. However, the thrill of my largest corporate achievement was quickly stifled. We all know that jealousy is an ugly monster and can make people stoop to conducting themselves in unflattering ways. Never in my dreams did I believe the success I'd brought to the company, would not be welcomed by everyone.

I felt like my life went from, "Hero" to "Zero" overnight. I now dreaded reading my emails as some were so troubling that I felt like a child being reprimanded for bringing home an A+ instead of an A++. While the employees were celebrating our accomplishments across the country, I was living in an isolated, uncomfortable environment.

Over the next 9 months, things went from bad to worse. There was nothing I could do or say, to make any difference. It seemed the better I performed, the more I allowed myself to focus on the negative reactions instead of celebrating the positive results. It became obvious to me I had to leave.

Have you ever heard the old adage, that you keep repeating the same lesson, until you've learned it? Well I'm living proof of that phrase. I quickly found myself in a partnership with a former employee of the company I'd left, to help build an international moving company. This time around I carried the, "CEO" title totally bypassing, "President" all together.

Barely two years spent with that corporation, found an employee using my business plans for a company he had on the side, an accountant who not only couldn't manage the finances properly, but also viewed the corporate bank account as a personal entitlement. For whatever reason I was on a 5 year streak, of keeping the wrong business people in my inner circle and I couldn't figure out why. It seemed every time I moved a little bit forward, those riding my coat-tail were setting up roadblocks and I was exhausted from jumping them.

One partner stopped coming to work, then quickly resigned 2 months later, leaving a wake of destruction. I spent 10 months repairing the damage that was done and working myself into a state of misery. How did I go from being a successful corporate princess to an uninspired, bitter individual? My family suffered and my friends worried about me. I had very little nice things to say and I just couldn't understand why this was happening to me. What did I do to deserve this? Why me and how the hell can I end this constant state of unhappiness?

There is no preparation for a breakdown. There's nobody telling you that you'll cry uncontrollably or beg out loud for help to dead air. More importantly, I had no one telling me that I could fix it myself. For all the different approaches I'd tried to 'fix' the negative situations, it never dawned, that I wasn't in control of how I reacted to them. I didn't know I had the power to accept or reject any situation, negative or positive in my life. I never viewed myself as the problem because it's so much easier to blame circumstances.

It all started with a decision. I remember the day when I decided I needed to focus on me first, before anyone else. It's ironic that I used to tell people, "you need to look after yourself before you can look after anyone else." Since I felt like I'd hit rock bottom, I needed to make myself the priority, that meant taking a good, long, look in the mirror.

I started to read books that helped me understand I am ultimately responsible for everything I have attracted into my life, plus how to focus on positivity. I needed to make myself accountable for the fear, pain, and anxiety I felt but held others responsible for. I needed to be Kirsten again, the strong business woman, the ultimate wife, the loving mother, the helpful friend, the comedian, everything. The world is a better place when I allow myself to be me.

My days start with a pen and journal. It's almost like talking to myself in a manner that I have no choice but to hear. I start by telling myself that I deserve the best in life, we all do. Then I make a list of things that I am truly grateful for. Sometimes, it's as simple as a breeze on a hot summer day or the heat from the wood stove, in the dead of winter. It doesn't matter what it is, it matters that I am grateful. Once I am topped up with gratitude, I send love to those who have hurt me. You read that right, I send them love. I have so much love to give and when I send that love to those who've hurt me, I forgive myself for allowing them to take my happiness away. The last thing I do is write out how I intend my day to be. A good example would be, "I am so happy and grateful now that my meeting with Mr. Smith was not only productive but, he also provided me a reference because he trusts my service." I will plan the perfect parking space, find the perfect dress or hear from an old friend. It is such a wonderful way to begin and has changed my life dramatically.

It was during this time and through a lot of soul-searching, I'd realized that I didn't want anyone else to feel as alone as I did during those bleak executive years. And so my journey to write a book began. "Underwater Boss," was written for men and women around the world who feel isolated in a tough business environment and can't see any way out. Ultimately, it is up to each individual to control their own life but I know my book will make them laugh, bring them comfort and hopefully, the courage to look for a better future.

This is an absolutely beautiful world we live in when we choose to see the beauty in it. Circumstances no longer control me. I am strong enough to decide which path is right for me and if I find it isn't serving me, then I make a course correction but never lose sight of my happiness.

Today, I recognize all the success I have achieved and am so proud of my accomplishments. I have set some really big goals for myself, ones that I have no idea how to reach and some that scare the daylights out of me but, I will not stop until I achieve them. I've seen the evil side of business and the ugly face of greed and vow to never participate in that again.

Life shouldn't be a struggle, don't let anyone tell you it should be. Enjoy your life, take charge of it, make this planet a better place to live, simply because you are in it. Invest in yourself first then help others.

Love,

Kirsten

Kirsten Flynn and her husband Randy live in rural Ontario. Together they've raised two beautiful daughters, Brenna and Dana. Kirsten has had a diverse career with many awards and achievements. She is the owner of a successful international moving company, Flynn International which enables her to travel the world. Kirsten was showcased on Undercover Boss Canada, which she still holds as one of the most honoured and humbling experiences of her life.

She is the author of "Underwater Boss, Drowning in Success" which is written with the purpose of letting career men and women know that they aren't alone in their corporate struggles and how they can break out of any negative relationship, by seeking the help of a mentor.

Visit www.myperfectmentor.com to connect with professional mentors and coaches from around the world. Kirsten is currently writing a second book on the lighter side of life, full of humour and shenanigans.

You can follow her journey at kirstenflynninternational.com.

16

BECOMING BEAUTIFUL
By Erika Jolene Gmeindl

"I use the pain to push me to greatness"

ERIC THOMAS

I think back to my childhood with compassion and understanding. It was a decade of anxiety, bullying, and shame. It was a series of moments that taught me I wasn't good enough because of my body. I remember wearing long, sleeved shirts on hot days so no one would make fun of my fat arms. I remember holding my stomach in, with hopes that no one would point it out. I remember hiding under portable stairs and having apples thrown at me, and I remember being terrified of gym class when my classmates would make fun of my body while I skipped, ran or jumped.

My saving grace was my beautiful, amazing mother. I would come home from school crying, and she would hold me and tell me all the reasons I was beautiful: I was kind, generous, compassionate, smart, and funny. She would explain that my classmates' harsh words were a result of ignorance and a lack of compassion on their part. I would eventually heal that night, and return to the same torture the following day.

By grade eight, I was two hundred pounds. I was fed up with being mistreated, and made the decision to lose the weight. From that moment on, I began making healthy choices. I was successful, and got lots of great feedback on my shrinking body! There was only one problem: my motivation for losing weight was that I wouldn't be good enough unless I did.

By the time I went to university I was 135 pounds, and although my body had changed, my **self-esteem** had not. I remember avoiding eye contact with my peers, and sitting in the music hall so I didn't have to eat in front of anyone. I remember having to get drunk just to be in social environments to feel confidence. It was also the only time I felt beautiful. I remember looking in every window I passed and feeling a wave of shame if I "looked fat" in any way, which I often did. My eyes would travel upwards and meet my wide-eyed, anxiety stricken, gaze. Then another wave of shame would slap my eyes back to the ground. My social anxiety cost me my university experience... I'd made only one friend in four years.

In my third year, I began teaching Pilates and muscle conditioning classes at the university, as well as at an adult dance studio. I loved being able to share my knowledge and passion with others! Above that though, I learned that being the facilitator of these classes afforded me the opportunity to create a non–judgemental, all-inclusive space in which people felt encouraged to move their bodies – no matter their size, shape or ability.

During my university years, I met a nutritionist named Steve, who helped me lose weight through self-compassion. He became my mentor and suggested I take a Fitness & Health Promotions program at a local college. I was accepted into the program, and at the same time, I was hired as a personal trainer at a boxing gym. Personal training was, (and still is) my dream career and I was over the moon to have a world champion boxer as my boss! He ended up teaching me as much about business as he did about boxing and for that, I will be eternally grateful.

My college years were considerably better than university. I clicked with my classmates and laughed my way through the two years. I was also able to take ideas and apply them to my personal training. It was an incredibly, effective educational experience that serves me to this day.

After college I was 135 pounds, still eating 1300 calories a day and working out one-two hours a day. I was still trying to lose weight. I remember slipping up often. I would eat 1000 calories over my quota one day and immediately jump on the treadmill with a full stomach. It was either that or hate myself the next day. Looking back now I can see that I had exercise bulimia, but at the time I just thought I was disciplined.

My slip-ups eventually turned into binges. I would eat quickly, not thinking about the smell or taste of my food. I often ate past the point of fullness, and sometimes past the point of pain. The next day not only did I feel shame, but my body got sore to the touch, feeling as if I had bruises all over. It always happened the day after a big binge, and it sometimes lasted a few days. I hated this feeling and tried to throw up on many occasions, but I just couldn't do it. Instead, I'd resume my exercise.

Soon came the evening of our annual family Christmas party and, like any Christmas party, there was food everywhere. I was determined not to eat junk that night, but after four hours of "white- knuckling" it, I gave in and had one cookie… then two… then four…then a tray. Then a tray of cheese and crackers. After everyone left I went upstairs in tears, hating myself for how sore I'd be tomorrow. I walked to the washroom and desperately shoved two fingers down my throat. Nothing. I wiggled. Nothing. I wiggled harder. I started to heave. And then it happened: it all came out. A smile took over my face and I cried tears of joy and relief. I didn't have to be in pain tomorrow. I didn't have to get fat because of my lack of willpower. I didn't have to feel shame. I sat down on the washroom floor in total disbelief. "A Christmas miracle," I thought.

A few months later, I'd met a guy and fell hard for him on our first date. On our third date, he invited me to his house for movies and wine. I could feel my anxiety rising thinking about him seeing or touching my body. I drank far too much that night and don't remember much except for a fuzzy memory of me crying on his bed, feeling not good enough. He lost interest after that night, and he ended it shortly after.

I was crushed, and hated myself for screwing it up. I began to binge every day. I would buy fast food, sweets, chips, and always ice cream, (it made everything taste better on the way up). I would sit in front of my computer, eating, and researching my disorder. When I felt pain from fullness I'd go throw up. Within half an hour I'd be eating again.

In four months I gained 40 pounds, which terrified me because I was fat again. Even more terrifying though, was the idea of letting go of my goal of losing weight, my value as a person depended on it! As terrified as I was, I was equally fed up with hating myself. I wanted to be happy, and was willing to do whatever it took to change that paradigm. At that moment I vowed not to lose any weight until I learned to love myself EXACTLY the way I was.

The next six months were tough. It was the summer, which meant I couldn't hide my newly found 40 pounds from my clients, my participants, or the mirrors that covered my gym. I was there from 6:30am-8:30pm and our gym's community looked up to me as a leader in health. I felt worthless.

If I wasn't with a client or class I was off crying. I'd fallen into a deep depression, and thought, "I'm nothing" over and over again. The crying was nothing like I'd experienced before. My sobs were deep and laboured, and it sounded like my soul was in pain. I'd try to rationalize losing just a bit of weight to make me feel more comfortable, and then I would let myself down gently. "No sweetie," I would tell myself, shaking in fear. "I'm sorry, but no."

As broken and tired as I was, I pushed myself to do absolutely everything I could to beat my paradigm. I did group therapy, counselling, and attended an online-facilitated meeting daily that taught C.B.T skills. I picked up every book on eating disorders and self-worth that I could find, including every book Geneen Roth had ever written. I reached out to my good friends. I journaled daily. I meditated daily. I let myself feel all the pain and trauma I had never let myself feel. I'd accepted the bullying at a young age, the self-imposed criticism throughout my life, and sincerely forgave all.

Then I began practicing affirmations and wrote positive, "I" statements on my mirrors with window markers. I would stand in front of my mirror naked, reading out the phrases, "I'm beautiful" and "I am enough." I would read them out through tears because I knew the last thing I was, was beautiful. I knew for a fact that I was fat, and that I was ugly, but I kept doing them anyway.

It was six months after my decision to love myself that I was walking past a department store window and caught my reflection. My first thought was, "I look good today!" I couldn't believe it, the affirmations had worked! I stopped and stared wondering who I was seeing. I looked closer, and for the first time, I didn't just see body parts. I saw a whole woman. I didn't feel shame or embarrassment. I wasn't trying to hide this or that. I was simply content with my appearance.

That moment marked the beginning of a love affair that will carry on for the rest of my life. For the first time I got to experience myself without my old paradigm, and I fell deeply in love with that woman. I came to know for a fact, that I was all the things my mom had seen in me as a child: kind, generous, compassionate, smart, and funny. In other words, I am absolutely beautiful.

Life became completely different. I was suddenly comfortable in social situations and eager to meet new people. I went to Atlantic City with 7 girls from my dance studio and spent my time on the beach in my bikini. I was the fattest one in the group, and I genuinely didn't care. In fact, that was the best I had ever felt at the beach in a bikini!

A month later I played, "Mas" at Caribana and shook my booty in front of thousands of strangers in a costume, which is basically a bikini! I was surrounded by all shapes and sizes jiggling everywhere! They had cellulite, they had fat, and they had sagging. They were smiling, they were glowing, they were free. And so was I. To date it was the happiest day of my life.

After a few months of enjoying my newfound freedom, I started to question why I'd developed an eating disorder. Sure, it was that I believed I wasn't good enough, but why did I believe that in the first place? I thought back to the children I had grown up with. How did they get the idea in their head that being fat was wrong, unacceptable? My first thought was the parents, but I highly doubted that 75% of my classmates' parents were teaching them to fat-bash.

I then thought back to all the TV I had watched over the years, all of the magazines and advertisements. Then I remembered an article I had read about children learning through pictures at a very young age. I then thought of the fact that children don't have the capacity to be media literate. This was the first time I saw the unhealthy cultural paradigm laid before our children. We as a society were indirectly teaching children through pictures that: a) being beautiful meant living up to particular physical requirements, and: b) For girls especially, this was one of the most important if not, the most important thing a woman can do to be socially accepted and valued.

It left me sick to think this is how our culture evolved, and sicker yet that the only way to change the social paradigm was to get corporations to change their media and advertising content. The latter only made me sick because I knew the only way companies would change their advertising was if they lost money over it. It would be impossible for me to make a difference to the corporations. I bowed my head in defeat and retired the idea.

It was no longer than a year later when I left the boxing gym and began training on my own. I made a good go at it, but I learned quickly that running a business meant you were on the clock 24/7, and you needed the passion for keeping that up. After what I'd gone through with my eating disorders I couldn't seem to find my passion again. At that time I decided to try out a few other jobs. I bounced around for a year and a half trying new things and found nothing I loved.

It was during that time I developed a healthy relationship with food, and with no intentions of doing so, dropped 20 pounds! I reintroduced the gym as a hobby and fell in love all over again. When I worked out it felt good, and it felt like me. I was quickly drawn to my personal training business again.

My passion and energy were contagious, and my clientele built up quickly. I was happy to be able to practice and use my business, social and fitness skills but, there was still something missing from my life. I had made such an amazing paradigm shift to unconditional self-love, and I wanted to give women the tools and guidance to do the same. I started a, "Women's Empowerment" group, and had 11 ladies sign up for my first lesson on self-acceptance. I continued to teach on topics of self-esteem and self-confidence, and acquired a following of fabulous women, many of whom have become my friend.

Although I was told I was making a difference, and I was walking away from workshops fulfilled, I still wasn't making an impact on a cultural level. It did not sit right with me, that all I was doing was fixing broken women. I wanted to prevent them from breaking in the first place.

That's when I began to fantasize about a revolution. I imagined seeing beautiful, vibrant women, like I had seen at Caribana on bus shelter advertisements. I envisioned girls looking through Cosmo and seeing diverse body types, and then imagined those girls learning that what you look like doesn't determine your worth. I envisioned children at school playing together, no matter their colour, height, body shape, body size, or anything else that had to do with appearance. Ultimately I was envisioning a culture in which children were bombarded with images of inclusion and acceptance, and therefore that is what they learned and practised.

I envisioned society's attitude change towards advertisements. I pictured a society that rejected the use of one body type in their media and ads for the sake of their children. I imagined sales and ratings going down and hitting bottom lines. I fantasized about corporations reforming to get their sales and ratings back up. I imagined a revolution in what our media reiterates to our children, and I imagined those girls and boys growing up with the deep understanding that all appearances are acceptable.

Even with my newfound self-love and earned confidence, I wasn't sure I could be the catalyst for such a revolution. It was a Thursday at noon when I first shared my secret desire with a group of friends during a master-mind meeting. I could barely get the words out, I felt embarrassed to admit I wanted to try for something so big. To my delight, I was met with love and support. It gave me the courage to go for it, and I began to write it down every day. I also wrote it on a card and put it in my wallet. It is still there to this day.

A month later, I remembered an idea I'd had about producing fitness panties. They'd be anti-bacterial, odour resistant, dry-fast fabric, and bright, neon colours with black trim. My mind raced. What if I could run a company that is the change I want to see in the media? What if I could lead by example through my advertisements? What if I could put a portion of my profits towards creating a revolution?

I fell in love with the idea and immediately found a fashion illustrator to draw my vision. I then brought my drawings to a pattern maker. She created a pattern which I took to a manufacturer in Toronto, and they created my samples. As of this moment, I am awaiting the newest sample in a thong cut.

Having never taken on a business plan and not having a degree in business, the process has been and continues to be a huge learning curve. I am learning on a personal level what it means to sacrifice friends, relationships, alcohol, etcetera, to become the person I need to be to complete my objectives. When I'm not training or teaching workshops, I am researching, networking, and refining my vision. When the workload and vision become overwhelming, which they often do, I remind myself that diamonds are formed under pressure – and to create the international social change I desire requires a diamond of a leader. More importantly than that, though, what really keeps me going is my vision of peace in the playground.

Dedicated to

Jane & John Gmeindl: *You are the reason I am who I am today. I would not have been able to be this person without your guidance, support, and your unconditional love. You two have been the best gift this world has given to me. From the bottom of my heart I thank you for everything you have sacrificed for my well-being and success. I love you both so much.*

Lindsay: *You have been my rock, my sounding board, my comic relief, and one of my biggest comforts in times of distress. Thank you for showing me what being a true friend means.*

Jeff & Lauren: *Thank you for your enthusiasm in Libella Panties, and all the work you've both put in so far. It touches me deeply to have you both invested in the vision, and I am so excited for our future!*

Neide, Melissa, Carrie & Sandra: *I just love you ladies. Thank you for showing me how strong we can become when us girls come together. You've shown me the true meaning of "Girl Power".*

Eric Thomas: *Because of you, I've become a better woman. I invite, and am thankful for criticism. I work hard to ensure my character won't take me down when my talent makes me soar. I take no days off and I've become allergic to average. Thank You for showing me how to become a diamond, and how to grind until I get there.*

Geneen Roth: *I call, "Women, Food & God" my "bible." It sits in a drawer beside my bed, and when my old paradigms pop up, I grab your book and am able to ground myself. Thank You for showing me what a healthy relationship with food, and with myself, looks like.*

Erika Jolene Gmeindl lives in Kitchener, Ontario where she runs her personal training business. Her days are filled with helping her clients get to their fitness goals in a healthy and balanced manner.

Erika's underwear company, Libella Panties, will launch later this year. Requests for pre-orders, information or queries on Erika's Women's Empowerment group can be sent to Erika's email directly: erikagmeindl@gmail.com.

Additional information on Erika's product line can be found on www.libella.ca.

17

YOUR WHITEBOARD OF LIFE

By Diane Gies

"This day that you're living right now is the only day you get. Period."

WAYNE DYER

I have always believed that my life was a journey. As a result, everyone that crosses my path becomes a part of my story. That excites me. I now know that every single experience and every encounter, good or bad, opens up the opportunity for me to learn a lesson and grow as an individual so that I can ultimately become a better wife, mom, daughter, friend.

I asked myself several years ago, "Diane, are you aware of your journey? Are you conscious of what you are experiencing?" To which I immediately responded, "of course I'm aware." I was aware that I had to wake up every morning to get my kids off to school. I was aware that I needed to go to work so that I could earn a paycheque to pay the mortgage and whatever other debts we had accumulated. I would come home, make dinner, get the kids off to dance and hockey, get some laundry in, pay some bills, have a glass of wine, watch one of my regular tv episodes and call it a night. So yes, I was definitely, "aware" of my journey. Or so I thought.

It was Saturday, August 14th, 2010 — a beautiful, sunny, summer day. Our typical Saturday where the kids were out playing by the pool, and I was doing the regular house chores that needed to get done for the day. It was 3:05pm when a call came in and my husband picked up from the home office. Within minutes he came back in the room, standing in front of me, staring blankly as though the life had just been sucked out of him. He was saying, "He's gone."

Not able to make sense of what he was saying, I ask, "What are you talking about? Who's gone?" In a frantic state he repeats himself, "He's gone... Jay is gone! They found him dead in his truck, shotgun beside him with self-inflicted wounds."

Jay is my husband's first-born child from a previous marriage, my stepson, the half-brother to my children. He left behind his 5-month-old baby boy and wife of 4 years. Just like that my life shifted. It was that very moment that my real journey began. The moment that ultimately opened my eyes to what I now refer to as my, "epic journey."

The moment my mind registered what had been said, I felt my body get sucked into what felt like a vortex. My life instantly became a movie that was playing in rewind mode, spinning backward at warped speed. My mind was going back in time. I tried to reconcile what I'd just heard, with any possible messages I may have received in my past, that would have warned me about this. There was nothing. My mind couldn't comprehend what had just happened. So now, I went into a frantic state. Once I overcame the initial shock, I went into a state of rage. I realized when one isn't able to understand what has just happened to them, they become angry.

You see, we go through the stages of grieving where being angry is normal. Only in my case, I was angry for 11 months after his death. I was angry at him for doing this to me. How dare he mess my life up like this! My life was no longer "normal." I now had to figure out what my new normal was going to be, and I blamed him for it. I blamed the world for my newfound misery and found myself playing the victim role because after all, I had totally convinced myself that this all happened to ME! I was being punished for something, but I didn't know what that something was.

After 11 months of having venom run through my veins, feeling the effects of all the toxins being produced from the anger, and the resentment I was hanging on to, I realized that my life was spiralling out of control. I wasn't living. I was merely existing, and knew at that point that I needed to regain control of my life.

It wasn't until I stopped to reflect on my life that I realized we are all born with what I refer to, metaphorically speaking, as a "Whiteboard." The Whiteboard actually represents your subconscious mind. This Whiteboard that we all come into this world with is a blank slate. There are no messages on there for us to use as a point of reference. We have no preconceived notions. We have no concept of right from wrong, nor the ability to judge. It is only when we expose our Whiteboard to the world that people begin to write messages on it, which ultimately begin to shape our destiny.

My parents were the first to leave messages on my board. While these messages helped shape and teach me right from wrong, good from bad, what to do and what not to do, they also left me believing things that weren't necessarily true. As I moved into my school years, my teachers left messages on my board. These messages helped teach me social etiquette and how to essentially behave in larger group settings, but again, left me with a set of beliefs that wouldn't necessarily serve me well in the future. I allowed my friends to write on my board, which left me with comments that quite honestly served no purpose, other than to make me question my self-worth.

These messages accumulated over time and eventually became my voice of reason. It was these messages that I referred to as an adult, which ultimately ended up governing my every thought and every move. These messages created my belief system. This belief system created my thoughts and those thoughts created my results.

You see, I believed that I was a victim of my circumstances and because of that belief, I wasn't able to see the lessons I was being offered through my experiences. The more I told myself I was a victim, the more evidence I seemed to find to support those thoughts, creating something known as a self-fulfilling prophecy.

I was raised in a home with two parents who lived tragic lives. Escaping from a communist country at a young age and seeing things that no child should ever see. They believed that people were the root of all evil and therefore, taught me to believe that I should trust no one. I was told that when bad things happened, it was because I was too excited and became over confident. I was taught to believe that success only comes when you have a lot of money and unless you have a significant amount of it, you wouldn't make it in life... nor make a difference in the world. This message was meant to motivate me and help me achieve success. Unfortunately, this was my father's definition of success, not mine.

My interpretation of that message left me with the belief that until I accumulated money and material goods, I would never be enough for people who did, in fact, have money. I would feel they were in a different class than me, and I had nothing significant to offer them. As a result, I had very few people in my life that I felt comfortable being around. I would meet people and question their intentions and I would certainly never get excited, for fear of getting hurt or disappointed. I would look into the future and base everything from past experience, finding myself always preparing for the worst. If I did in fact attempt to deviate from my belief system and all that I had been taught, I would feel guilty for disappointing someone or fear being judged. If I failed at something, it was yet another message that was added to my, "Whiteboard" reminding me to never do it again.

I knew in my heart at a very young age that I was destined to make a difference in the world and my story would somehow change lives, but my belief system never allowed me to pursue my dreams. Rather than use my imagination and focus on what I wanted in life I would focus on what I didn't have, creating a vicious cycle that continued to bring me more of the same, which was nothing more than misery and disappointment. I was in constant pursuit of happiness and no matter how "successful" I became as an adult, I found myself always looking for more.

I had everything, a home, career, husband, two beautiful children, all the makings of a "successful" life, yet I felt like I had nothing. How was this possible? How do you have everything yet feel like you have nothing at all? I did everything I was supposed to do and still, I found myself in a pool of misery. I would find myself hoping and wishing that one day things would be different, waking up the next day only to find the same scenario as the day before.

It wasn't until I was faced with yet another challenge in my life, this one being something no parent should ever have to face. The day had finally come where my 17-year-old boy, born with a congenital heart disease was required to go in for open-heart reconstructive surgery. Knowing that he was facing his own mortality, I couldn't bear to accept that he may not come back to me. It was not an option. It was the moment we parted, when he was wheeled through the doors of the operating room. It was then, I realized I needed to **Believe, not Hope nor Wish, but BELIEVE**.

That very moment I noticed my life shift. It wasn't until I made the decision to look at my beliefs, that had been created from the messages on my, "Whiteboard" that I was able to create new messages that were aligned with my heart's desire. In order to create the new messages, I needed to first go back and erase the old ones. It started with my desire. The desire to have my son come out alive and live his life as he was meant to live it. That desire outweighed any negative belief I had about being a victim, about the world conspiring against me, or even that I was being punished.

There was nothing more in life I wanted at that very moment, then to have my son come back to me. Nothing. I knew I could not merely hope or wish that he would come back to me, I had to **BELIEVE**. So be it and so it was.

As I reflected on that moment in time, I began to apply that philosophy to everything in my life. I erased all the messages on my Whiteboard that prevented me from Believing. All the experiences that would make me question whether I could achieve my hearts desires. I no longer wish or hope, but rather **Believe** that everything that I create in my mind will come to fruition. It is only when you attach the strongest of emotions to your vision that you will receive exactly what you desire.

I have learned in life that it is imperative to use every single experience that comes your way and try to find the lesson that is being given to you. I now know that my stepson did not die in vain. While he may not have felt he had a voice while here in physical form, he certainly has a voice now… through me.

My son was born with a congenital disease for a reason, to teach me that when you want something bad enough, leave no room for any other option, you will get what you set your mind to. Because of his experience, he is now touching lives of all people who cross his path. He now knows that he was born with a gift and he is not a victim but rather a hero to all who are blessed to know him.

You see, our lives really are made up of a tapestry of events that ultimately create one incredible journey. So while your final destination may seem exciting, it truly is the journey and all of its events… good and bad that we have to be thankful for today. After all, today is all that we have, so let's make it epic!

Diane is a Facilitator and Coach. She specializes in raising awareness of the role we play in creating our own reality. A graduate of the social work program, she has dedicated her life to understanding human behaviour and ultimately creating change where change is needed.

As a result of many years of research and studying the needs of individuals, Diane is now offering **Elite Wellness Retreats** that directly impact the mind, body and soul. She has partnered with specialists in several sunny destinations to create epic adventures for all walks of life. You can find more information on how these retreats can be customized to meet your needs by visiting www.ewgetaways.com.

Diane lives with her family in Waterloo, ON where she continues to work as a Personal Development Coach. A mother of two beautiful teenagers, she claims have taught her everything she knows and attributes her success to them. She hopes to one day travel more extensively to underprivileged countries, and do what she loves most, give back.

Until then, Diane will continue to share her love for people through her work as a coach and trainer. Diane can personally be reached at diane@dianegies.com.

18

MY MIRACULOUS JOURNEY
From Near Death To Internationally Recognized Coach
Triumph in Six Months
By Mariett Ramm

In the 15 months since my heart attack and near-death experience in an Italian ICU on August 30, 2015, I have made a massive quantum leap in all areas of my life. That medical catastrophe happened on the exact day that Wayne Dyer, one of the authors I most admire, suffered a fatal heart attack. How ironic! (It turns out that Wayne Dyer actually guided me to find Bob Proctor, my inspiration and mentor). It took me three weeks of doing almost nothing except sleeping and eating to recover from the heart attack. I had many ECGs, X-rays, blood tests, medications, and other forms of emergency care during that time. My body was giving up. It was as if I had lived three lifetimes in my 36-year-old body.

I was literally lost, looking for something that I couldn't even define. I started listening to the world renowned Bob Proctor, also referred by many as, "The Godfather Of Personal Development." His teachings were on YouTube and I was captivated wanting to learn more. I decided to contact his company with my personal information. Within a very short period of time, I'd been given an appointment with a sales representative. He actually became a very dear friend. We talked for an hour while I ranted about where I was in life, and what I wanted to do. He asked me, "How would you like to meet Bob Proctor? We've got a big seminar coming up next month in Toronto."

By April 2016, I had gotten off the alcohol and drug addiction that I had escaped into and used as a crutch to mask the pain of personal and professional losses. I would drink three bottles of wine a day, smoke hash, bit of coke, coffee, tobacco, junk food — you name it.

I also suffered badly with bulimia and anorexia, which were ongoing for 24 years. That eating disorder manifested for me about 7 times in a typical day, during which I'd take more than 20 laxatives to purge myself and drink 10 litres of water to flush my stomach out. After mistreating my body for over two decades, there was no withdrawal, no clear concise treatment plan.

The thought of meeting Bob Proctor in Toronto was like a light bulb going on. I immediately said yes, not giving any consideration to the fact that I was petrified of flying. Ever since my heart attack the previous year, I had refused to get on an airplane. I did not want to be any place where I felt enclosed. However in this instant, I had agreed and didn't think about the fact that I would be on an airplane for eight hours from Europe to Toronto. I then started to work on myself and my mindset, based on Bob's material. I arranged some short trips on airplanes to accustom myself to flying again. I went back to the UK after a year and a half.

I also did a trip to Hungary, my birth country. I was born during the era of communism. It was a chaotic time, a time of paradigms and communist beliefs. I was an only child. My mother put me on a pedestal but had become very overprotective. This was the result after I'd suffered abuse at the hands of a religious leader. I was only twelve years of age at the time. That started the development of my eating disorder which lasted more than half my life. I was left with the impression that I was, "good for nothing" and would never amount to anything. Because of my family background, it was a difficult decision to finally visit my family in Hungary, to make amends over the several years of silence. I knew I had to do it for my own peace of mind.

These new travel experiences and expectations gave me the feeling that something good was really going to happen in my life, at last.

By the beginning of July, I was really ready. I organized my trip to Toronto, with two fabulous days of sightseeing. To say that I was full of excitement is an understatement. I went to a five-day event known as the, "Matrixx" presented by Proctor Gallagher Institute. I met Bob Proctor, his business partner Sandy Gallagher, some of the most wonderful, supportive people on their team, and other seminar attendees.

I've never been in such an electric environment before, such high levels of expectation. It was all I had hoped for. I was finally becoming awake. My energy was coming back. I felt free, my spirit was opening. I had the confidence that I could do anything. I was becoming alive, but more importantly, I was becoming the real me.

On the second day that week, I decided to enroll in the company's coaching program. I joined PGI as a consultant! This was it! This was exactly what I'd been seeking, although I hadn't known it. The program, the teaching, my life experience, the way it suddenly all unfolded, was phenomenal. I was ecstatic to have this opportunity. It satisfied me and gave me a purpose.

I finally understood that everything I had gone through that had been so painful, needed to be experienced, in order for me to come to this point. I took it all as a sign that I was on the right path. I believe that everything comes into our lives for a reason, and all this was just one more sign of that truth. I finally had a clear picture of the trajectory my life had been on. In fact, Bob Proctor often quotes Steve Jobs, who talks about how one can only connect the dots of his or her life by going backward.

The week I'd spent at the "Matrixx" changed the course of my life! I had learned about goal setting; that until I could change my mindset I would not be able to get out of the prison I was in. I had to relearn to think, instead of medicating myself with drugs and alcohol.

I'd realized that my purpose was to share my entire life journey - the lessons I've learned, the addictions, the loss of loved ones, the sexual abuse, the self-abuse, the relationship abuse, being jobless and broke. To share this with thousands of people and possibly affect their future decisions positively, that knowledge was mind-blowing!

Personal losses and disappointments? Yes. One of my first major relationships was extremely turbulent. I felt like nothing more than a housemate who would cook, iron, and clean. It was a hostile, toxic environment. I learned a lot of difficult lessons during that time and lost my identity as a person.

My next loss occurred when my wonderful marriage ended, as my husband died of cancer in 2011. He was my soulmate, best friend, and true partner. Losing him was devastating. In 2013, I lost my one and only friend to suicide as well as my business. I truly hit rock bottom.

But...

From July 2016, I was now in the reconstruction stage of my new life. It seemed that I was going to impact so many people as I came to life again at a higher plateau, than I had ever reached before. I am so happy and thankful the Universe conspired to give me this rare opportunity. I spent a month digging into the mindset material, trying to understand the lifetime of programming I had gone through and these big changes that were suddenly happening now. Then I opted to attend a private event for 15 people, the 1% Club, in Hawaii in mid-August. I wanted to spend more time with Bob Proctor getting to know myself, and the new direction that I was drawn toward.

The attendees were very successful people such as CEOs, millionaires, and business people. I wanted to understand how their mindsets correlated with their business activities. They were searching for more than just material success.

Then I experienced real doubts: What was I doing here? I had nothing to show for my life and wanted to crawl back into my shell. Soon after a one-on-one with Bob, my whole self-image changed. I think Bob was a bit put out by my sob story at first. Then he saw I was serious and told me that if I wanted to be a coach, I needed to follow a course of action. I had to go to the Far East to study. I made a decision then and there to spend a month in Bangkok, learning about developing my business.

Bob was speechless, astounded, and most amazed. He told me that in the 55 years of his career, he had never seen anyone make such a precise and definite decision so quickly. You know the story when Andrew Carnegie timed Napoleon Hill to agree to write, Think And Grow Rich? It took Hill 27 seconds to decide. I think I took about 5 seconds. I knew I had absolutely nothing to lose, and everything to gain. I finally saw my path.

So I went back to Europe, back to living by myself, and focused on becoming a Bob Proctor coach. I started cold-calling business people. I noticed the extreme contrast in optimism for the people coming into my life and the people I knew from before. They were dynamic, positive and creative. It was a beautiful, inspiring change.

I realized that my frequency level had changed, and I was embarking on a different life. I continued working on my website, studying, listening to Bob Proctor and reading. I could see and experience myself as being a coach, attracting a different type of client because I wanted to.

Then, I went to Bangkok for a month and had many revelations there. I learned about my true purpose from a "Healer" whom I spent 5 hours with at a go! I had deep insights of my own having to think into the results I wanted, with no help what-so-ever, in a country where they hardly speak English. I learned that when what you believe, is aligned with behavior, that's when the magic happens! I learned about the Law of Attraction and Universal Vibration. I learned about pushing through real fears. I understood that when we start to live our lives working with the Laws of the Universe, the force we are aligned with is just amazingly powerful.

I could see myself sharing my recovery experiences with thousands of appreciative people. I could be valuable to society! I could be proud of what I'd accomplished and where I came from. I was developing a different awareness of situations and circumstances, both past and present. I wanted to build a business that was very different from what I'd done before, and much more efficient in its operation. Case in point: I am now an internationally recognized T.I.R. consultant (Thinking into Results). I am being contacted by CEOs globally about team-building and mentoring.

In December 2016, my photo graced the front cover of a new upmarket global branding magazine, 'MilliOnAir', along with my story inside. I have a dynamically growing social media platform on LinkedIn, Facebook, and Twitter. I am becoming an expert on multiple sources of income (MSI), networking, and creating several businesses. Through the miraculous workings of the Universe, I have also been put in touch with one of the most prestigious addiction clinics in the U.K. I have great plans to fulfill my personal desire to help and encourage addicts, by using my own recovery based on the most valuable works, I was fortunate to attract into my life.

Another example of the effortless and growing change in my business life happened several months ago. I encountered a network professional, who has become a magical friend. The Universe sent her to open many doors, resulting in introductions to like-minded, growth oriented, individuals, company owners, and global corporations requiring my training.

I honestly feel that I am a true testament and Messenger from Spirit. I had to experience before I could move on with my purpose. Experiencing is learning, and it is creating. Failure and heartache is phenomenal because it shows that we are going into unchartered territory. We are learning. We are growing. I am so happy and grateful for my past, that enabled me to experience, and I would not change a single thing.

I also learned that once the conscious mind gives up, out of the blue the solution to the problem appears. Whether it's the light bulb or the iPhone or the Internet, that's the way things happen. Oftentimes, there is no rational explanation for the success of major business ideas. Trust and faith are keys to understanding.

When I realize how far I've come since that awful day in August 2015, when I nearly lost my life to a heart attack, I truly give thanks. Now I'm on a clear path to being a well-respected coach and consultant with interesting and dynamic clients all over the world. It seems like a miracle, but really, it's just one more sign of what can happen when you follow the path of where you are truly meant to be.

Mariett Ramm is a globally recognized Mentor, Speaker, and Inspirational Figure. Mariett is also a contributor of **MiliOnAir**, **Huffington Post**, and global platform **Richtopia** which is a popular read with iconic influencers like Richard Branson. Mariett runs her own seminars, "**Made In The Mind**" in Central London. She also offers online courses for anyone who is interested in achieving results with mindset combined with skill sets, and income strategies. www.mariettramm.com

Mariett's contact information:

- **Facebook**: Mariett Ramm
- **Twitter**: @mariettramm
- **LinkedIn**: Mariett Ramm
- **Skype**: Mariett.Ramm2
- **Website**: www.mariettramm.thinkingintoresults.com

19

BEGINNING WITH ONE THING
By Jay Whitelaw

"Make no little plans; they have no magic to stir men's blood."

DANIEL BURNHAM

"Wake up every day and do one thing that will take you closer to reaching your goal." That was the simple, yet profound advice that I'd received from a good friend of mine as I sat paralyzed in a local coffee shop. For some reason, this advice made sense and cut through the other competing voices in my head. The next day I sent a simple email and the terrifyingly, awesome journey began.

Thirteen years before the coffee shop challenge, the seed had already been planted. I had flown to Namibia, Africa to volunteer as a teacher for 12 months in a small town called, Grootfontein. There, I met a man named Kamati and, through him, learned what it was really like to give. I watched him give out from the little he had, and was moved by his joy of giving. To exercise what I was learning, I emailed my friends back home to see if together, we could help Kamati purchase a mattress to sleep on and a small fridge to store food in his house. We raised the money in a matter of days. After making the purchases and doing something nice for my new friend, I imagined that would be it. I couldn't have been more wrong.

Within the hour, word spread that Kamati had been cared for. I quickly found myself in the middle of a "Namibian-style" dance celebration, that rocked me to the core. As the community celebrated the kindness of the gesture, I had realized, it was the first time in my entire life that I had been able to see the tangible impact of a charitable donation. It was my friends' money, but there I was, watching with my own eyes the difference it had made, not only for Kamati but for the entire community around us. It brought me to tears witnessing a simple gesture having such a profound impact. It left me with an undeniable burden to do something about it. Eventually, I did… 11 years later.

I was at a conference in Las Vegas, minding my own business when a simple video and a complete stranger changed the direction of my life forever. We were in a 60-minute team-building exercise, building prosthetic hands for people who required them. Initially, a woman at my table resisted taking part, preferring to join a different room where she could, "actually learn something." She was quite upset and very angry that she was being made to participate. And then it happened. After completing the hand, a video was played. It showed the same hands we'd just made, being distributed and attached to grateful people around the world. We got to witness the hands being used and the reactions from those receiving them. It was incredibly emotional. I looked at the angry woman to see if this mattered to her. What I saw was a broken, sobbing, transformed individual. Through tears, she turned to me and said, "I can't wait to go home and tell my family what just happened, because this just changed my life!"

And in one sentence she changed mine. My internal wrestling match was over. I knew I needed to do something about this. She reminded me of my experience in Namibia by showing me the incredible compassion of the human heart, when we're given the chance to see the difference we make when we give. I decided that day, I was going to create an opportunity where anybody could give a few dollars to a charitable project. I would then provide them with real video footage, to witness for themselves the true impact of their gift. Which brings me to the coffee shop, where I sat, caught in a battle of unbelievable excitement and unimaginable fear.

I had decided to go for it, but I was stalling. The idea was too big for me. I was not an entrepreneur. I had no expertise. I didn't know the first thing about starting a not-for-profit. Then I heard it again. "Wake up every day and do one thing that will take you closer to reaching your goal." It resonated with me. It was something I knew I could do.

I didn't know the full picture and I didn't know how I was going to accomplish it. The unknowns and the sheer size of the task overwhelmed me. But I knew I could do one thing. Who can't do one thing? It removed the pressure, made it seem possible, and was the inspiration I needed to take my first step. I woke up the next day and sent an email. The day after that I sent another one. Then I had coffee with someone. Every day I took one step forward. Then I started taking two steps. I felt the momentum building and the excitement and belief started to overtake the fear.

I was writing goals and reading them out loud. I was walking in faith, believing there was something bigger happening here. I was asked to be the keynote speaker at a community event on giving, so I said yes. I was invited to meet with a CEO, so I went for it. Every day I kept moving closer, choosing to live outside my comfort zone, accepting challenges as they came, and gaining momentum every week.

Now, I look back at that terrified person in the coffee shop and I don't recognize him. So much has changed since starting this journey. If I could go back and whisper three things to myself, having learned what I've now learned, this is what I'd say.

1. Don't wait until it's safe and don't wait for all the answers... Just go.

Looking back, I realize that it was impossible for me to have known then, what I now know before beginning the journey. What you need to know and who you need to know will enter the picture only once you start to move. As a cautious and calculating person, this drove me nuts. I've learned that standing on the starting line does nothing to add to your experience or wisdom. You must first walk. If you are compelled by an idea or a vision, in order to give it any hope of coming to life, you must begin to move and act.

I can remember the week I started moving forward, I had my first dentist appointment at a new clinic in town. When the hygienist, who was making small talk, asked me what I did for a living. I desperately wanted to describe my previous job. Instead, I said, "I'm the founder of a non-profit called Givesome and we show people around the world the difference they make when they give." It was my first time ever answering this way. I thought she might call me on it, but you know what she did? She took off her mask, pulled up a chair and asked me to tell her more. We talked for several minutes and she was fascinated. I've never wavered in my responses ever since. You don't need safety and you don't need all the answers... you just need to move.

2. Face the fear, and the fear goes away.

I've found that the best way to face fear is to move toward it. In doing so the unknown becomes known. The questions get answered. The people you need to help you come into the picture and the work you need to accomplish gets completed. Fears are best addressed as you move towards them. What used to scare me has now lost its power.

I used to fear the thought of presenting Givesome to wise and influential CEO's. What if they ask me questions I don't know the answers to? What if I can't clearly communicate my message? What if they think I'm out to lunch? The remedy I chose, was to book meetings with hundreds of them. Literally! I've travelled across the country discussing Givesome with some of the most influential CEO's and leaders in Canada and now there's no more fear. It would be difficult to ask a question now, that I've not already been asked a hundred times.

The more you face what it is you fear the smaller that fear becomes. Stop running from it, or in my case, stop being paralyzed by it. Move towards your fears and they will help produce some of your greatest assets.

3. Develop a crystal-clear goal that produces an image that excites you.

What I've come to love about goals is how customizable and personal they are. My goals may not move someone else, but when I read and imagine them, it's like a giant shot of adrenaline in the arm. This is an important step and not to be overlooked. We've heard the saying, "Aim at nothing and you'll hit it." Setting a goal is your opportunity to ensure that what you seek to achieve becomes achievable.

One of my favorite exercises, especially in the early days, was writing, reading and re-writing my goal until it perfectly described exactly what I was after. It made any decision making very easy because I knew exactly what I was building.

One of the tremendous highlights that I experienced along the journey was watching what I clearly saw in my imagination begin to take shape in reality. Create it first in your imagination and then build it in real life. For over a year I built Givesome in my imagination and on paper, in sketches and over conversations. Then I went out and created it again in real life.

For those who find themselves in the proverbial coffee shop, excited but fearful, wanting to move forward but having no clue how, I share with you what a wise man once shared with me. "Wake up every day and do one thing that will take you closer to reaching your goal." Buckle up! It'll be the best ride of your life.

Jay Whitelaw lives in Guelph, Ontario with his wife Hannah and son Jackson. After 10+ years in the experiential training industry he left to pursue his passion for charity and to encourage a new kind of giving. It's one that connects with people at a heart level, showing givers the true difference they make when they give. Jay is the Founder and Executive Director of Givesome Foundation (2015).

He has created the Givesome app, which provides users with an opportunity to fund tangible projects for small amounts of money, then receive video footage of project completion right to their mobile device. Givesome is in partnership with several national companies and is being used as a unique utility for employee and customer engagement in businesses across Canada. When he's not traveling or speaking, Jay enjoys tennis, hockey and impromptu wrestling matches with his son.

Learn More:
- Web: www.givesome.ca
- Twitter: @givesome_gives
- Instagram: givesome_gives
- FB: givesomegives
- Email: admin@givesome.ca

20

MISTAKEN IDENTITY

By Doug Dane

"It's not what you are that is holding you back. It's what you think you are not."

DENIS WAITLEY

Everyone wakes up, eventually!

For me, it was a cool, sunny morning in April 2003 when my life story appeared on the front page of the Toronto Star. I decided that I needed to go public with my story because I'd been struggling for so long. I needed to normalize the leftover emotions from the trauma and abuse I had endured.

I remember waking up that morning, picking up the newspaper afraid and excited about how people would react. What would they think? What would they say? How would they view me? What would they think of me?

Most of the questions came from an inbred fear of criticism growing up in a violent, abusive, alcoholic family.

The days following the article were a whirlwind of support, responses from others who were struggling and massive movement of emotions mixed with relief, confusion, and strength. The healing came at a remarkable rate! Feelings of shame, worthlessness, and fear fell away like a heavy yoke carried on my shoulders.

It took me another 10 years of study, counselling, and introspection to fully realize the impact of my childhood experiences and programming. It was late 2012 and I found myself in another depression, feeling lost and purposeless. Questions kept running through my mind. Why am I here? What is my purpose? What am I supposed to be doing with the rest of my life? I felt my story had a bigger reason and bigger purpose but my self-image kicked in and reminded me, "Who are you to think you are special or have something important to do?"

One morning, something compelled me to watch the movie The Secret, and Bob Proctor came on the screen barking at me in his fatherly, wise voice. You become what you think about, you're responsible for your life and your results, you can be, do, or have anything you want!

Twenty-three years earlier, I had attended a Bob Proctor weekend seminar. It literally changed the course of my life, but I had forgotten most of what I had learned and as Bob's voice rang in my ears, it all came flooding back. That's when I realized I had been living with a mistaken identity.

We've been programmed!

When we were young our parents told us what was right and what was wrong. They taught us to be good and punished us if we were bad. They instilled rules and beliefs and our identity was formed. But, it's a mistaken identity because it was their rules, their values, and their beliefs. They were handed down to them by their parents. We were programmed to believe things about ourselves and the world, that just aren't true.

When I was little I listened and learned and watched. When we are young we don't have the ability to choose our beliefs. We listen to our parents and our teachers and our family and as we get programmed we act like the person we are told to be. The reactions we get from our actions confirm, that is who we are.

For me, it was very confusing watching my alcoholic Dad, beat on my Mom, my beaten Mom would beat on me. I was left trying to figure out what was normal. Was it normal that I was told to lie about what was going on at home? Was it normal that I felt weak and confused? Was it normal that I didn't feel loved? Was it normal that I needed validation and approval? Why did I think there was something wrong with me?

I had realized, it all started for me when I was given away at birth. I was the fifth of six kids given away by my birth mother. If I could ask the question when I was a baby, "What's wrong with me, why are you giving me away?" I know she would've said, "because it's what's best for you." But as a young child, knowing I was given up and adopted, it left me with the feeling I must be damaged.

I was damaged! My mom had beaten me with her hands and a strap, but also with her words. Her violent, beer stenched mouth would spew out hate and disgust but then when she was sober, there were some glimpses of love and warmth. There are very few memories I hold of connection, love, validation or approval. As I searched for the foundation of emotional strength that all kids need and I deserved, I was left to figure out who and what I was.

At the age of twelve, my Mom left home for good, my father a broken and now sober man spent his days in this lazy-boy chair, eating frozen dinners and trying to figure out where he went wrong. My father's mistaken identity was handed to him from a generation of violence and alcohol. It's no wonder he did what he did, it's what he knew, it's how he was programmed, it's what he believed about himself. What a terrible way to go through life!

Searching for validation and approval, I fell into the clutches of a ring of pedophiles and I was sexually abused for two years. It ended in my kidnapping at fifteen and again I was left to figure out why this happened. What was wrong with me? And why did I feel the way I did about myself? How could I do something so wrong?

My mistaken identity continued to build. That's how our self-image is formed. We believe the things we are told, we experience events in our life, we make mistakes trying to get it right and because they are facts, we see ourselves in the image that was created. Our self-image holds us back - mine sure did! Nobody's perfect right? We are all perfect as we are, the only thing that is wrong with us, is the concept we have of ourselves.

My mistaken identity was like a tight-fitting coat. It was itchy and uncomfortable and didn't feel right. I've carried this feeling inside since I can remember, that there was something special about me, that I had gifts to share, that I'd landed in the wrong family and that who and what I had become wasn't ME.

Our programming does that. Something feels off, it doesn't quite feel right. We feel like there is something missing. We have a desire to be more, do more and have more. We have this sense that we were meant for something more but our self-image holds us back.

"Your self-image sets the boundary of individual achievement."

MAXWELL MALTZ, AUTHOR OF
PSYCHO-CYBERNETICS

My self-image was sure holding me back. I had a desire to help people and teach people what I had learned about success, making money and goal achievement. After watching The Secret, I had this feeling that I was supposed to help other people free themselves from what was holding them back - themselves. In fact, I spent 10 years after my story was in the newspaper and on television thinking about what I wanted to do. But each time, I started to seriously entertain the idea that I could be a successful speaker and coach, my self-image would kick in and talk me out of it. My mistaken identity kept causing me to look back on where I had come from.

Stop looking backward!

Your self-image is a tricky thing to change if you don't understand how much it's controlling your life. Whatever you think about is what you become. "As a man thinketh in his heart, so is he."

The identity I held of myself held me back from going after what I really wanted, but I didn't understand why or how. I spent years looking back on my past. I spent years in counselling trying to deal with the residue of my past. I kept looking back on all the mistakes I had made, thinking about the people I had hurt in my relationships and listening to those blabbering voices in my head reminding me of who I thought I was.

Whatever you focus on and think about is who and what you become. If you keep looking backwards then that is how you will see yourself and you will keep acting like the person you see. This was a big lesson for me. When it hit me I finally made sense of why I was stuck and kept making the same mistakes over and over.

Let go of the past!

"Let it go," my mentor said, "just forget about it." Easy for you to say, I thought to myself. I had tried for years to let go of the past but I couldn't! I tried, believe me, I tried! What a frustrating feeling knowing I could let go, but I wasn't. It seemed every time things would be getting better my self-image would kick in and pull me back. It felt like I was climbing a mountain with a thick rope around my waist. I was trying to climb to the top to my dreams and goals but, the weight of my past around my waist kept pulling me back. Two steps forward, 3 steps back dammit!

Then I discovered what was holding me back. My mistaken identity was comprised of my self-image, the beliefs I had about myself and others, and the events that had taken place in my life. My mentor said the events of your past have made you who you are and has led you to this point. Everything that has happened to you, happened for a reason. I began to evaluate my beliefs about myself and I discovered most of them were just not true. I had spent years believing they were true and acting on those beliefs. When you evaluate your beliefs you can change your beliefs.

My beliefs were holding me back. They were like sandbags on the basket of a hot air balloon. All I wanted to do was fly, to be free and soar. As I took inventory of my beliefs I replaced them with new beliefs, and it was like cutting the ropes on the sandbags and I began to take off.

The key to letting go was to reprogram myself with my own beliefs. I was speaking to a client of mine and she wanted to multiply her income in her business. She had always struggled with earning money. I started asking her some questions about what her parents told her about money, and what she was told about herself when she was young. As we began to dig into her beliefs, she discovered her beliefs about money weren't true, and how she saw herself in business was a mistaken identity created by her father. She told me she was speaking with her parents about her desire to become wealthy. She told me her Dad said, "We didn't raise you that way." I told her, wouldn't it be great if we could go back and tell our parents to raise us the way WE want to be raised.

As you discover who you really are, what you're meant to be, you'll realize the only thing holding you back is how you see yourself. Look in the mirror, the image you see is a reflection of light of the outer image of yourself. The inner image, the concept of yourself was programmed into you and you have the ability to program yourself. And so that's what I did!

"If I want to be free, I gotta be me."

My mentor kept quoting one of his mentors' sayings "If I want to be free, I gotta be me. Not the me I think you think I should be, but the me I want to be."

When we were raised we developed a fear of criticism. At first, we were taught what was right and wrong and good and bad. Then if we were good we were praised and loved and if we were bad we were punished, and made to feel small. We felt judged! I watched my parents judging others. They taught me to judge myself and then I began judging others and when others judged me, I would shrink and hide.

I couldn't figure out why I was so uncomfortable around people. The second-guessing and lack of confidence kept eating away at me. Why was I so confused and scared? Why did I feel like I didn't know where my life was going? I was a walking contradiction. I felt like a hypocrite. Why did I feel so unauthentic? Because I wasn't being me! The inbred fear of criticism, caused me to continue to act like the person I thought everyone wanted me to be. I was always worried about what everyone was thinking about me and I realized they weren't. My mentor said to me, "Doug, you'll stop worrying about what other people think about you, when you realize they very rarely do." He said, "If you stop thinking about yourself, you won't find anything wrong with yourself." Wow, that really hit me!

I had spent so many years worrying about what others thought of me and what I thought of myself. I realized I was self-centred and kept thinking about myself. I'm not self-centred with others. I've always put others ahead of me but I spent a lot of time thinking about myself, and what was wrong with me. And then I realized there was nothing wrong with me. The only thing that was wrong, was how I saw myself. And my concept of myself was my mistaken identity. So many of us are imprisoned because of a mistaken identity. The key to freedom is to look inside at who you really are. There's nothing wrong with you. It's your job to figure out who and what you are.

How do you want to be known?

That's a good question, isn't it? That's the question I began to ask. It leads to more questions. How do I want to see myself? How do I want to feel about myself? What makes me happy? What do I love to do? I can be and do anything I want! I often wonder if I had landed in a different family, who I might have become. No doubt another mistaken identity, maybe a better one or maybe worse.

Every once in a while you meet someone who soars in life. They make it look easy. They are very confident and clear on who and what they are. They know their purpose and they know their why. I think some land in the right place when they arrive here, and the programming they receive matches up with who they really are, and they just feel right!

I think most of us struggle with our identity. For me, it was a lifelong struggle trying to figure out why I felt the way I felt. But now, I know I am the master of my fate and the captain of my soul. I can create my life to be any way I want and I can become the person I was destined to become. I'm finding the peace and beauty in conscious living because now I'm being the me I want to be and I'm finally free!

How do I want to be known? I'm a leading example that no matter where you are or where you came from, you can create a beautiful life. A life with purpose, one that matters and one that helps others. I was put here to share my story to inspire others to break free from their past and their mistaken identity. And I'm doing it each day. I love what I do! I love who I'm becoming and finally, I'm beginning to love myself!

Doug Dane has been called a cognitive authority on self-image.

In April 2003 Doug went public with his life story and it appeared on the front page of The Toronto Star newspaper. Since then he has had a remarkable ride. Doug has appeared on national TV with Canada AM, he was featured on TV Ontario's Person 2 Person program with Paula Todd and his story is featured in her best-selling book, "A Quiet Courage."

Today he is a successful entrepreneur, coach, and keynote speaker. Doug is a consultant working alongside Bob Proctor. Bob calls Doug, The "Stuckbuster", he's an expert at getting people unstuck.

Doug is the proud father of his daughter Eden and lives in Guelph ON.

Visit his website at www.dougdane.com

Email: doug@dougdane.com

21

BUILD IT YOUR WAY

By Claudette Snow

"You Are Confined Only By The Walls You Build Yourself"

ANDREW MURPHY

I hope somewhere among these pages, you found cause to reflect on your own life, your existence, and your purpose. There is a wealth, of knowledge, life-lessons and raw honesty expressed here.

Life isn't always easy and it doesn't always go as planned. In fact, I would say that's the beauty of living. How would we ever learn a lesson or gain any valuable insights if everything went well? How would we know true love if we'd never had heartache and how would we discover how to improve ourselves if we never made mistakes?

Life is about continuously course correcting in order to discover where we want to be, how we want to be and who we want to be. It's not an easy thing to figure out, yet there isn't any one person who can make the choices for your life, except for you. Not if you want to be happy at least.

Have you ever taken the time to ask yourself if you are truly living? Are you happy with your lifestyle, your friends, and your income? While these questions may seem trivial to some, they are disturbing to others. That's because the majority of people don't live the life they want and they are totally unaware of how to attain it.

As children, we all had dreams of being someone special, a doctor, rock star, lawyer, astronaut, a princess perhaps. We talked about travelling the world and having all kinds of magical adventures. We never even had to think about money because, well you just knew we were all going to be as rich as kings. Those sure were the days. We were young, wild and free to think and dream anything we wanted. We had it all right there in our imaginations.

So, what in the hell happened?!

Are you living the life you had dreamed for yourself or did you just take the first available opportunity that came your way? Are you happy or are you settling for what is easy? If you could do anything you wanted, would you be doing what you are doing right now?

Why did we lose sight of our dreams and goals? Every person has a different answer but few admit the real reason. Most will blame their situation on circumstances or other people. It's so much easier to place blame outside ourselves than to take responsibility for our own existence. I was no different. I had to hit rock bottom in my life before I realized that I had a choice in how I wanted to live my time here on earth. I had allowed others to determine my position, value, and self-worth. Guess what? That's not a wise thing to do.

While my life appeared to be a fairy tale to those looking in, I suffered silently yearning to be who I dreamed of being, who I knew I was. I'd never let go of my childhood fantasy, but I'd never openly pursued it either. Why? I knew you'd ask. I was afraid. I was afraid I would fail. I was afraid I'd be judged. I was afraid I was too old to pursue my dreams. It's hard to admit but, my biggest fear was being afraid of succeeding.

It took me quite a while to understand that I had a right, to live my life my way. I had always thought that every other person's wants, needs, dreams, and desires were more important than my own. I couldn't seem to figure things out by myself, so I had to reach out to someone who could make me see the truth.

It was very difficult for me to explain to someone that I really wanted more than I had. I knew I had to do it though. I knew deep down inside that I hadn't been living the life I was meant to live. I knew I held gifts within me that I wanted to share. I knew I could help others by being myself.

I wasn't exactly certain who could help me with my situation, but I quickly learned that having a **trained mentor**, likely saved me a fortune in therapy. My mentor was quick to identify my issues and teach me how to overcome any obstacles on my path. I learned a different way of thinking and gained an education that will serve me in every aspect of my life, for many years to come. He taught me about fear and how it can keep you stuck and prevent you from moving forward.

Something amazing happens when you face your fears and chase your goals. Your entire life starts to change and evolve into everything you always knew was possible. You end up building the life you always wanted, only now you build it your way. You take control and make decisions. You feel inspired and excited to know that there is still time. You feel joy at knowing that those who were meant to be on your journey will stay and support you. You will attract everyone and everything needed to make your dream a reality.

Where there's a strong desire, there's a way and all things are possible. We need to believe in our goals. We need to believe in ourselves. Once we move toward the thing we are meant for, all kinds of doors start to open for us. Have faith in yourself and climb over the fear.

If you can't figure it out on your own, then ask someone who knows how to get you there. You are no less than anyone else. Whatever you want, you can have. If you truly want something, nothing will prevent you from having it. When you dig deep inside and realize how very special each and every one of us truly is, you would never cast doubt on achieving your dreams. You can have the life you want. Whether it be health, wealth or relationships, you have the ability to attain it.

I never want to leave this earth with any regrets. I want to see as much as I can. I want to travel and experience every opportunity and I want to help as many people as possible become the best version of themselves. I want to make a difference in the world and I want to leave a legacy behind. That requires me to move forward, chase my dreams and build more. And, you know what? There's a pretty simple way to do that.

Ask, **Believe** and **Receive**.

"Start today. Start building the life you want and build it your own way."

CLAUDETTE SNOW

ACKNOWLEDGEMENT OF GRATITUDE

As the wee hours of the morning unfold, the calmness of darkness fills my soul. The moon shining bright, the stars twinkling magically in Morse Code across this miracle of a universe. The message is heard and I know it's time to wrap up this big dream of mine. It's time to express my gratitude to those who made this book come true.

First and foremost, I thank my family for their support and patience throughout the creation of this book. I especially thank my talented daughter Emily Weimer for her feedback, technical wizardry, and computer skills. Without her assistance, I'd likely be sitting here 3 years from now trying to figure things out.

There have been so many incredible people who assisted me on my journey through these pages. My contributing authors are some of the most amazing, skilled and gifted individuals I've ever had the privilege to meet. I thank each of you for your kindness, professionalism and support. Most of all, I thank you for sharing your stories and experiences with the world. Together, we are motivating and inspiring others to reach higher, dream bigger, and BELIEVE in themselves. Thank you for changing lives and showing others what is possible through your own achievements. It is an absolute honour to be affiliated with those who leave an impression of increase with everyone around them.

Thank you to Jeff Davad Photography for providing me with promotional shots and allowing me to experience a nervous but fun day in your studio.

David Morrison, words will never be enough to express how grateful I am to have you in my world. You are the finest example of what humanity should be. Just so you know, you're never getting rid of me.

For everyone who played a role, big or small in encouraging me through this often nerve-racking journey, I thank you from the bottom of my heart.